Hands-On MQTT Pr[...]
with Python

Work with the lightweight IoT protocol in Python

Gaston C. Hillar

BIRMINGHAM - MUMBAI

Hands-On MQTT Programming with Python

Commissioning Editor: Kunal Choudhari
Acquisition Editor: Reshma Raman
Content Development Editor: Aditi Gour
Technical Editor: Sushmeeta Jena
Copy Editor: Safis Editing
Project Coordinator: Hardik Bhinde
Proofreader: Safis Editing
Indexer: Tejal Daruwale Soni
Graphics: Jason Monteiro
Production Coordinator: Shraddha Falebhai

First published: May 2018

Production reference: 1180518

Published by Packt Publishing Ltd.
Livery Place
35 Livery Street
Birmingham
B3 2PB, UK.

ISBN 978-1-78913-854-2

www.packtpub.com

`mapt.io`

Mapt is an online digital library that gives you full access to over 5,000 books and videos, as well as industry leading tools to help you plan your personal development and advance your career. For more information, please visit our website.

Why subscribe?

- Spend less time learning and more time coding with practical eBooks and Videos from over 4,000 industry professionals

- Improve your learning with Skill Plans built especially for you

- Get a free eBook or video every month

- Mapt is fully searchable

- Copy and paste, print, and bookmark content

PacktPub.com

Did you know that Packt offers eBook versions of every book published, with PDF and ePub files available? You can upgrade to the eBook version at `www.PacktPub.com` and, as a print book customer, you are entitled to a discount on the eBook copy. Get in touch with us at `service@packtpub.com` for more details.

At `www.PacktPub.com`, you can also read a collection of free technical articles, sign up for a range of free newsletters, and receive exclusive discounts and offers on Packt books and eBooks.

About the Author

Gaston C. Hillar is Italian and has been working with computers since he was 8 years old. Gaston has a bachelor's degree in computer science (graduated with honors) and an MBA. He is the CTO of Mapgenix, a freelance author, and a speaker.

He has been a senior contributing editor at Dr. Dobb's and has written more than a hundred articles on software development topics. He has received the prestigious Intel® Black Belt Software Developer award eight times.

He lives with his wife, Vanesa, and his two sons, Kevin and Brandon.

Acknowledgements:

While writing this book, I was fortunate to work with an excellent team at Packt, whose contributions vastly improved the presentation of this book. Reshma Raman allowed me to provide her ideas to write a book dedicated to MQTT programming with Python, and I jumped into this exciting project. Aditi Gour helped me realize my vision for this book and provided many sensible suggestions regarding the text, the format, and the flow. The reader will notice her great work. It's been great working with Reshma on another project and I can't wait to work with Reshma and Aditi again. I would like to thank my technical reviewers and proofreaders for their thorough reviews and insightful comments. I was able to incorporate some of the knowledge and wisdom they have gained in their many years in the software development industry. This book was possible because they gave valuable feedback.

The entire process of writing a book requires a huge number of lonely hours. I wouldn't be able to write an entire book without dedicating some time to play soccer against my sons, Kevin and Brandon, and my nephew, Nicolas. Of course, I never won a match. However, I did score a few goals! Of course, I'm talking about real-life soccer, but I must also include virtual soccer when the weather didn't allow us to kick a real-life ball.

About the reviewer

Ben Howes is the founder and lead consultant at Zoetrope Ltd, a specialist IoT consultancy and product development firm in the UK. Ben has been creating connected hardware for over 10 years and has worked across projects spanning from start-ups to multinational deployments.

I'd like to thank Richard Webb, my cofounder, for starting Zoetrope with me.

Packt is searching for authors like you

If you're interested in becoming an author for Packt, please visit `authors.packtpub.com` and apply today. We have worked with thousands of developers and tech professionals, just like you, to help them share their insight with the global tech community. You can make a general application, apply for a specific hot topic that we are recruiting an author for, or submit your own idea.

Table of Contents

Preface

MQTT is the preferred IoT publish-subscribe lightweight messaging protocol. Python is definitely one of the most popular programming languages. It is open source, multiplatform, and you can use it to develop any kind of application. If you develop IoT, web applications, mobile apps, or a combination of these solutions, you must learn how MQTT and its lightweight messaging system works. The combination of Python and MQTT makes it possible to develop powerful applications that communicate with sensors, different devices, and other applications. Of course, it is extremely important to take security into account when working with this protocol.

Most of the time, when you work with complex IoT solutions coded in modern Python 3.6, you will use different IoT boards that might use diverse operating systems. MQTT has its own specific vocabulary and different working modes. Learning MQTT is challenging, because it includes too many abstract concepts that require real-life examples to be easy to understand.

This book will allow you to dive deep in to the latest version of the MQTT protocol: 3.1.1. You will learn to work with the most recent Mosquitto MQTT server, command-line tools, and GUI tools to allow you to understand how everything works with MQTT and the possibilities that this protocol provides for your projects. You will learn security best practices and use them for a Mosquitto MQTT server.
Then, you will work with many real-life examples in Python 3.6. You will control a vehicle, process commands, interact with actuators, and monitor a surf competition by exchanging MQTT messages with the Eclipse Paho MQTT client library. You will also work with a cloud-based, real-time MQTT provider.

You will be able to run the examples on a wide range of modern IoT boards, such as Raspberry Pi 3 Model B+, Qualcomm DragonBoard 410c, BeagleBone Black, MinnowBoard Turbot Quad-Core, LattePanda 2G, and UP Core 4GB. However, any other board that supports Python 3.6 will be able to run the samples.

Who this book is for

This book is aimed at Python developers who want to develop applications that can interact with other applications and devices, such as IoT boards, sensors, and actuators.

What this book covers

Chapter 1, *Installing an MQTT 3.1.1 Mosquitto Server*, starts our journey toward the usage of the preferred IoT publish-subscribe lightweight messaging protocol in diverse IoT solutions, combined with mobile apps and web applications. We will learn how MQTT and its lightweight messaging system work. We will understand the MQTT puzzle: clients, servers (formerly known as brokers), and connections. We will learn the procedures to install an MQTT 3.1.1 Mosquitto server in Linux, macOS, and Windows. We will learn special considerations for running a Mosquitto server on the Cloud (Azure, AWS, and other cloud providers).

Chapter 2, *Using Command-Line and GUI Tools to Learn How MQTT Works*, teaches us to work with command-line and GUI tools to learn how MQTT works in detail. We will learn MQTT basics, the specific vocabulary for MQTT, and its working modes. We will use different utilities and diagrams to understand the most important concepts related to MQTT. We will understand everything we need to know before writing Python code to work with the MQTT protocol. We will work with the different Quality of Service levels, and we will analyze and compare their overheads.

Chapter 3, *Securing an MQTT 3.1.1 Mosquitto Server*, focuses on how to secure an MQTT 3.1.1 Mosquitto server. We will make all the necessary configurations to work with digital certificates to encrypt all the data sent between the MQTT clients and the server. We will use TLS, and we will learn to work with client certificates for each MQTT client. We will also learn to force the desired TLS protocol version.

Chapter 4, *Writing Code to Control a Vehicle with Python and MQTT Messages*, focuses on writing Python 3.x code to control a vehicle with MQTT messages delivered through encrypted connections (TLS 1.2). We will write code that will be able to run on different popular IoT platforms, such as a Raspberry Pi 3 board. We will understand how we can leverage our knowledge of the MQTT protocol to build a solution based on requirements. We will learn to work with the latest version of the Eclipse Paho MQTT Python client library.

Chapter 5, *Testing and Improving Our Vehicle Control Solution in Python*, outlines using our vehicle control solution with MQTT messages and Python code. We will learn how to process commands received in MQTT messages with Python code. We will write Python code to compose and send MQTT messages with commands. We will work with the blocking and threaded network loops, and we will understand the difference between them. Finally, we will take advantage of the last will and testament feature.

Chapter 6, *Monitoring a Surfing Competition with Cloud-Based Real-Time MQTT Providers and Python*, gets you started with writing Python code to use the PubNub cloud-based, real-time MQTT provider in combination with a Mosquitto MQTT server to monitor a surfing competition. We will build a solution from scratch by analyzing the requirements, and we will write Python code that will run on waterproof IoT boards connected to multiple sensors in surfboards. We will define the topics and commands, and we will work with a cloud-based MQTT server, in combination with the Mosquitto MQTT server used in the previous chapters.

Appendix, *Solutions*, the right answers for the *Test Your Knowledge* sections of each chapter are included in the appendix.

To get the most out of this book

You need a basic knowledge of Python 3.6.x and IoT boards.

Download the example code files

You can download the example code files for this book from your account at www.packtpub.com. If you purchased this book elsewhere, you can visit www.packtpub.com/support and register to have the files emailed directly to you.

You can download the code files by following these steps:

1. Log in or register at www.packtpub.com.
2. Select the **SUPPORT** tab.
3. Click on **Code Downloads & Errata**.
4. Enter the name of the book in the **Search** box and follow the onscreen instructions.

Once the file is downloaded, please make sure that you unzip or extract the folder using the latest version of:

- WinRAR/7-Zip for Windows
- Zipeg/iZip/UnRarX for Mac
- 7-Zip/PeaZip for Linux

The code bundle for the book is also hosted on GitHub at https://github.com/PacktPublishing/Hands-On-MQTT-Programming-with-Python. In case there's an update to the code, it will be updated on the existing GitHub repository.

We also have other code bundles from our rich catalog of books and videos available at https://github.com/PacktPublishing/. Check them out!

Download the color images

We also provide a PDF file that has color images of the screenshots/diagrams used in this book. You can download it here: http://www.packtpub.com/sites/default/files/downloads/HandsOnMQTTProgrammingwithPython_ColorImages.pdf.

Conventions used

There are a number of text conventions used throughout this book.

CodeInText: Indicates code words in text, database table names, folder names, filenames, file extensions, pathnames, dummy URLs, user input, and Twitter handles. Here is an example: "Mount the downloaded WebStorm-10*.dmg disk image file as another disk in your system."

A block of code is set as follows:

```
@staticmethod
    def on_subscribe(client, userdata, mid, granted_qos):
        print("I've subscribed with QoS: {}".format(
            granted_qos[0]))
```

When we wish to draw your attention to a particular part of a code block, the relevant lines or items are set in bold:

```
time.sleep(0.5)
    client.disconnect()
    client.loop_stop()
```

Any command-line input or output is written as follows:

```
sudo apt-add-repository ppa:mosquitto-dev/mosquitto-ppa
```

Bold: Indicates a new term, an important word, or words that you see onscreen. For example, words in menus or dialog boxes appear in the text like this. Here is an example: "Select **System info** from the **Administration** panel."

Warnings or important notes appear like this.

 Tips and tricks appear like this.

Get in touch

Feedback from our readers is always welcome.

General feedback: Email `feedback@packtpub.com` and mention the book title in the subject of your message. If you have questions about any aspect of this book, please email us at `questions@packtpub.com`.

Errata: Although we have taken every care to ensure the accuracy of our content, mistakes do happen. If you have found a mistake in this book, we would be grateful if you would report this to us. Please visit `www.packtpub.com/submit-errata`, selecting your book, clicking on the Errata Submission Form link, and entering the details.

Piracy: If you come across any illegal copies of our works in any form on the Internet, we would be grateful if you would provide us with the location address or website name. Please contact us at `copyright@packtpub.com` with a link to the material.

If you are interested in becoming an author: If there is a topic that you have expertise in and you are interested in either writing or contributing to a book, please visit `authors.packtpub.com`.

Reviews

Please leave a review. Once you have read and used this book, why not leave a review on the site that you purchased it from? Potential readers can then see and use your unbiased opinion to make purchase decisions, we at Packt can understand what you think about our products, and our authors can see your feedback on their book. Thank you!

For more information about Packt, please visit `packtpub.com`.

1
Installing an MQTT 3.1.1 Mosquitto Server

In this chapter, we will start our journey toward using the preferred IoT publish-subscribe lightweight messaging protocol in diverse IoT solutions, combined with mobile apps and web applications. We will learn how MQTT and its lightweight messaging system work.

We will understand the MQTT puzzle: clients, servers (formerly known as brokers), and connections. We will learn the procedures to install an MQTT 3.1.1 Mosquitto server in Linux, macOS, and Windows. We will learn special considerations for running a Mosquitto server in the cloud (Azure, AWS, and other cloud providers). We will gain an understanding of the following:

- Understanding convenient scenarios for the MQTT protocol
- Working with the publish-subscribe pattern
- Working with message filtering
- Understanding the MQTT puzzle: clients, servers, and connections
- Installing a Mosquitto server on Linux
- Installing a Mosquitto server on macOS
- Installing a Mosquitto server on Windows
- Considerations for running a Mosquitto server in the cloud

Understanding convenient scenarios for the MQTT protocol

Imagine that we have dozens of different devices that must exchange data between themselves. These devices have to request data from other devices, and the devices that receive the requests must respond with that data. The devices that request the data must process the data received from the devices that responded with the required data.

The devices are **Internet of Things (IoT)** boards that have dozens of sensors wired to them. We have the following IoT boards with different processing powers:

- Raspberry Pi 3 Model B+
- Qualcomm DragonBoard 410c
- Udoo Neo
- BeagleBone Black
- Phytec phyBoard-i.MX7-Zeta
- e-con Systems eSOMiMX6-micro
- MinnowBoard Turbot Quad-Core

Each of these boards has to be able to send and receive data. In addition, we want a web application to be able to send and receive data. We want to send and receive data in near-real time over the internet, and we might face some network problems: our wireless networks are somewhat unreliable and we have some high-latency environments. Some devices have low power, many of them are powered by batteries, and their resources are scarce. In addition, we must be careful with the network bandwidth usage because some of the devices use metered connections.

 A metered connection is a network connection where we have a limited amount of data usage per month. If we go over this amount of data, we get billed extra.

We can use HTTP requests and build a publish-subscribe model to exchange data between different devices. However, there is a protocol that has been specifically designed to be lighter than the HTTP 1.1 and HTTP/2 protocols. The **MQ Telemetry Transport (MQTT)** is better suited for a scenario in which many devices have to exchange data between themselves in near-real time over the internet and we need to consume the least network bandwidth possible. This protocol works better than HTTP 1.1 and HTTP/2 when unreliable networks are involved and connectivity is intermittent.

The MQTT protocol is a **machine-to-machine (M2M)** and IoT connectivity protocol. MQTT is a lightweight messaging protocol that works with a server-based publish-subscribe mechanism and runs on top of **TCP/IP (Transmission Control Protocol/Internet Protocol)**. The following diagram shows the MQTT protocol on top of the TCP/IP stack:

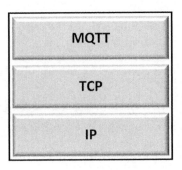

 The most popular versions of MQTT are 3.1.1 and 3.1. In this book, we will work with MQTT 3.1.1. Whenever we reference MQTT, we are talking about MQTT 3.1.1, the newest version of the protocol. The MQTT 3.1.1 specification has been standardized by the OASIS consortium. In addition, MQTT 3.1.1 became an ISO standard (ISO/IEC 20922) in 2016.

MQTT is lighter than the HTTP 1.1 and HTTP/2 protocols, and therefore it is a very interesting option whenever we have to send and receive data in near-real time with a publish-subscribe model, while requiring the lowest possible footprint. MQTT is very popular in IoT, M2M, and embedded projects, but it is also gaining presence in web applications and mobile apps that require assured messaging and an efficient message distribution. As a summary, MQTT is suitable for the following application domains in which data exchange is required:

- Asset tracking and management
- Automotive telematics
- Chemical detection
- Environment and traffic monitoring
- Field force automation
- Fire and gas testing
- Home automation
- **In-Vehicle Infotainment (IVI)**
- Medical
- Messaging
- **Point of Sale (POS)** kiosks

- Railway
- **Radio-Frequency Identification (RFID)**
- **Supervisory Control and Data Acquisition (SCADA)**
- Slot machines

As a summary, MQTT was designed to be suitable to support the following typical challenges in IoT, M2M, embedded, and mobile applications:

- Be lightweight to make it possible to transmit high volumes of data without huge overheads
- Distribute minimal packets of data in huge volumes
- Support an event-oriented paradigm with the asynchronous, bidirectional, low-latency push delivery of messages
- Easily emit data from one client to many clients
- Make it possible to listen for events whenever they happen (event-oriented architecture)
- Support always-connected and sometimes-connected models
- Publish information over unreliable networks and provide reliable deliveries over fragile connections
- Work very well with battery-powered devices or require low power consumption
- Provide responsiveness to make it possible to achieve near-real-time delivery of information
- Offer security and privacy for all the data
- Be able to provide the necessary scalability to distribute data to hundreds of thousands of clients

Working with the publish-subscribe pattern

Before we dive deep into MQTT, we must understand the publish-subscribe pattern, also known as the pub-sub pattern. In the publish-subscribe pattern, a client that publishes a message is decoupled from the other client or clients that receive the message. The clients don't know about the existence of the other clients. A client can publish messages of a specific type and only the clients that are interested in that specific type of message will receive the published messages.

The publish-subscribe pattern requires a *server*, also known as a **broker**. All the clients establish a connection with the server. A client that sends a message through the server is known as the **publisher**. The server filters the incoming messages and distributes them to the clients that are interested in that type of received messages. Clients that register to the server as interested in specific types of messages are known as **subscribers**. Hence, both publishers and subscribers establish a connection with the server.

It is easy to understand how things work with a simple diagram. The following diagram shows one publisher and two subscribers connected to a server:

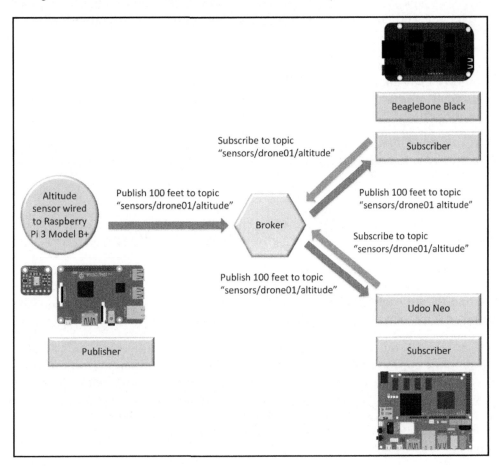

A **Raspberry Pi 3 Model B+** board with an altitude sensor wired to it is a publisher that establishes a connection with the server. A **BeagleBone Black** board and a **Udoo Neo** board are two subscribers that establish a connection with the server.

The **BeagleBone Black** board indicates to the server that it wants to subscribe to all messages that belong to the **sensors/drone01/altitude** topic. The **Udoo Neo** board indicates the same to the server. Hence, both boards are subscribed to the **sensors/drone01/altitude** topic.

 A *topic* is a named logical channel, and it is also referred to as a channel or subject. The server will send subscribers only messages published to topics to which they are subscribed.

The **Raspberry Pi 3 Model B+** board publishes a message with **100 feet** as the payload and **sensors/drone01/altitude** as the topic. This board, that is, the publisher, sends the publish request to the server.

 The data for a message is known as the **payload**. A message includes the topic to which it belongs and the payload.

The server distributes the message to the two clients that are subscribed to the **sensors/drone01/altitude** topic: the **BeagleBone Black** and the **Udoo Neo** boards.

Publishers and subscribers are decoupled in space because they don't know each other. Publishers and subscribers don't have to run at the same time. The publisher can publish a message and the subscriber can receive it later. In addition, the publish operation isn't synchronized with the receive operation.

A publisher requests the server to publish a message, and the different clients that have subscribed to the appropriate topic can receive the message at different times. The publisher can send a message as an asynchronous operation to avoid being blocked until the server receives the message. However, it is also possible to send a message to the server as a synchronous operation with the server and to continue the execution only after the operation was successful. In most cases, we will want to take advantage of asynchronous operations.

A publisher that requires sending a message to hundreds of clients can do it with a single publish operation to a server. The server is responsible for sending the published message to all the clients that have subscribed to the appropriate topic. Because publishers and subscribers are decoupled, the publisher doesn't know whether any subscriber is going to listen to the messages it is going to send. Hence, sometimes it is necessary to make the subscriber become a publisher too and to publish a message indicating that it has received and processed a message. The specific requirements depend on the kind of solution we are building. MQTT offers many features that make our lives easier in many of the scenarios we have been analyzing. We will use these different features throughout the book.

Working with message filtering

The server has to make sure that subscribers only receive the messages they are interested in. It is possible to filter messages based on different criteria in a publish-subscribe pattern. We will focus on analyzing *topic-based* filtering, also known as subject-based filtering.

Consider that each message belongs to a topic. When a publisher requests the server to publish a message, it must specify both the topic and the message. The server receives the message and delivers it to all the subscribers that have subscribed to the topic to which the message belongs.

The server doesn't need to check the payload for the message to deliver it to the corresponding subscribers; it just needs to check the topic for each message that has arrived and needs to be filtered before publishing it to the corresponding subscribers.

A subscriber can subscribe to more than one topic. In this case, the server has to make sure that the subscriber receives messages that belong to all the topics to which it has subscribed. It is easy to understand how things work with another simple diagram.

The following diagram shows two future publishers that haven't published any messages yet, a server, and two subscribers connected to the server:

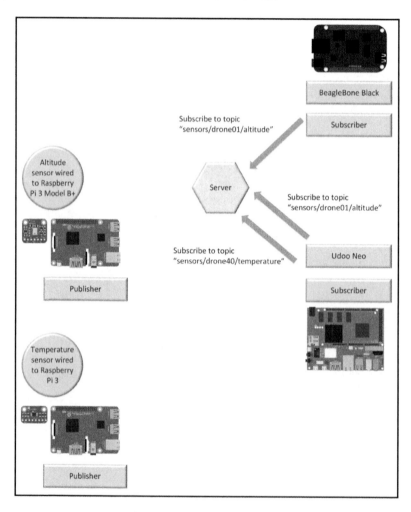

A **Raspberry Pi 3 Model B+** board with an altitude sensor wired to it and a **Raspberry Pi 3** board with a temperature sensor wired to it will be the two publishers. A **BeagleBone Black** board and a **Udoo Neo** board are the two subscribers that establish a connection to the server.

The **BeagleBone Black** board indicates to the server that it wants to subscribe to all the messages that belong to the **sensors/drone01/altitude** topic. The **Udoo Neo** board indicates to the server that it wants to subscribe to all the messages that belong to either of the following two topics: **sensors/drone01/altitude** and **sensors/drone40/temperature**. Hence, the **Udoo Neo** board is subscribed to two topics while the **BeagleBone Black** board is subscribed to just one topic.

The following diagram shows what happens after the two publishers connect and publish messages to different topics through the server:

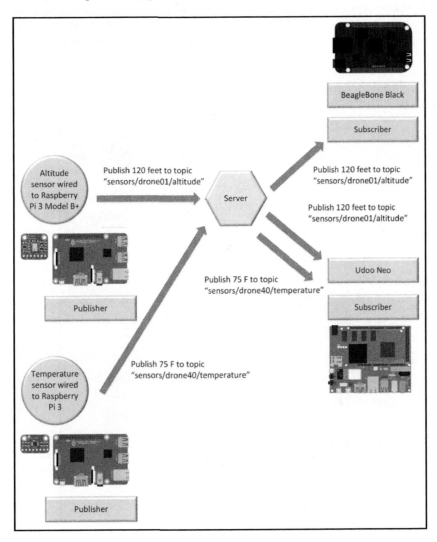

The **Raspberry Pi 3 Model B+** board publishes a message with **120 feet** as the payload and **sensors/drone01/altitude** as the topic. The board, that is, the publisher, sends the publish request to the server. The server distributes the message to the two clients that are subscribed to the **sensors/drone01/altitude** topic: the **BeagleBone Black** and the **Udoo Neo** boards.

The **Raspberry Pi 3** board publishes a message with **75 F** as the payload and **sensors/drone40/temperature** as the topic. The board, that is, the publisher, sends the publish request to the server. The server distributes the message to the only client that is subscribed to the **sensors/drone40/temperature** topic: the **Udoo Neo** board. Thus, the **Udoo Neo** board receives two messages from the server, one that belongs to the **sensors/drone01/altitude** topic and one that belongs to the **sensors/drone40/temperature** topic.

The following diagram shows what happens after one publisher publishes a message to a topic through the server, and this topic has only one subscriber:

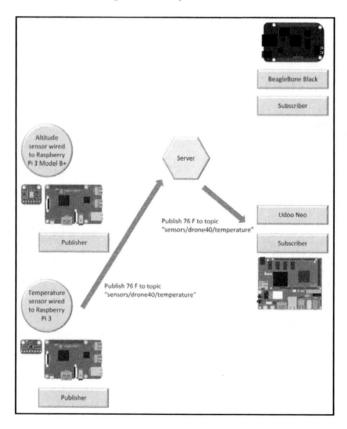

The **Raspberry Pi 3** board publishes a message with **76 F** as the payload and **sensors/drone40/temperature** as the topic. The board, that is, the publisher, sends the publish request to the server. The server distributes the message to the only client that is subscribed to the **sensors/drone40/temperature** topic: the **Udoo Neo** board.

Understanding the MQTT puzzle – clients, servers, and connections

In versions of the MQTT protocol lower than 3.1.1, the MQTT server was known as an MQTT broker. Starting in MQTT 3.1.1, the MQTT broker was renamed the MQTT server, and therefore we will refer to it as the server. However, we must take into account that the documentation for MQTT servers, tools, and client libraries can use the old MQTT broker name to refer to the server. MQTT servers are also known as message brokers.

The MQTT server uses the previously explained topic-based filtering to filter and distribute messages to the appropriate subscribers. There are many MQTT server implementations that provide additional message filtering features by providing custom plugins. However, we will focus on the features that are part of the MQTT protocol requirements.

As previously explained, in MQTT publishers and subscribers are completely decoupled. Publishers and subscribers are MQTT clients that only establish a connection with the MQTT server. An MQTT client can be both a publisher and a subscriber at the same time, that is, the client can publish messages to specific topics and also receive messages that belong to topics to which the client has subscribed.

There are MQTT client libraries available for the most popular programming languages and platforms. One of the most important things that we must consider when we select the MQTT client library is the list of MQTT features that they support and the ones that we need for our solution. Sometimes, we can choose between many libraries for a specific programming language and platform, and some of them might not implement all the features. We will use the most complete libraries for modern Python versions that support a wide range of platforms throughout the book.

Any device that has a TCP/IP stack and is capable of using an MQTT library can become an MQTT client, that is, a publisher, a subscriber, or both a publisher and a subscriber. The MQTT library makes it possible for the device to talk to MQTT on top of TCP/IP and to interact with specific types of MQTT server. For example, any of the following can become an MQTT client, among other devices:

- An Arduino board

- A Raspberry Pi 3 Model B+ board
- A BeagleBone Black board
- A Udoo Neo board
- An iPhone
- An iPad
- An Android tablet
- An Android smartphone
- A laptop running Windows
- A server running Linux
- A MacBook running macOS

There are many MQTT servers available for the most popular platforms, including Linux, Windows, and macOS. Many of them are servers that can work as MQTT servers and they also provide additional futures. An MQTT server might implement only a subset of the MQTT capabilities and might have specific limitations. Hence, it is very important to check all the capabilities we will require in our solution before selecting an MQTT server. As happens with other middleware, we have open source versions, free versions, and paid versions. Thus, we also have to make sure we select the appropriate MQTT server based on our budget and our specific needs.

Throughout this book, we will work with the Eclipse Mosquitto MQTT server (http://www.mosquitto.org). Mosquitto is an open source MQTT server with an EPL/EDL license that is compatible with MQTT versions 3.1.1 and 3.1. We can take advantage of everything we learn with any other MQTT server, such as **Erlang MQTT Broker (EMQ)**, also known as Emqttd (http://www.emqtt.io), and HiveMQ (http://hivemq.com), among others. In addition, we might use our knowledge to work with a cloud-based MQTT server such as CloudMQTT (http://www.cloudmqtt.com) or the PubNub MQTT bridge (http://pubnub.com). We will specifically work with cloud-based MQTT providers too.

The MQTT server is the central hub of the publish-subscribe model we previously analyzed. The MQTT server is responsible for the authentication and authorization of the MQTT clients that will be able to become publishers and/or subscribers after they are authenticated and authorized. So, the first thing that an MQTT client must do is to establish a connection with the MQTT server.

In order to establish a connection, the MQTT client must send a CONNECT control packet to the MQTT server with a payload that must include all the necessary information to initiate the connection and proceed with the authentication and authorization. The MQTT server will check the CONNECT packet, perform authentication and authorization, and send a response to the client with a CONNACK control packet that we will analyze in detail after understanding the CONNECT control packet. If the MQTT client sends an invalid CONNECT control packet, the server will automatically close the connection.

The following diagram shows the interaction between an MQTT client and an MQTT server to establish a connection:

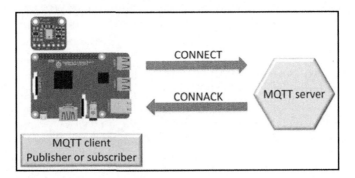

After a successful connection has been established between an MQTT client and an MQTT server, the server will keep the connection open until the client loses the connection or sends a DISCONNECT control packet to the server to close the connection.

The CONNECT control packet must include values for the following fields in the payload, and bits for a special flags byte that is included in the control packet. We want to understand the meaning of these fields and flags because we will be able to specify their values when we work with MQTT tools and MQTT client libraries in Python:

- ClientId: The client identifier, also known as client ID, is a string that identifies each MQTT client that connects to an MQTT server. Each client that connects to the MQTT server must have a unique ClientId, and the server uses it to identify the state that it holds related to the MQTT session between the client and the server. If a client specifies an empty value as the ClientId, the MQTT server must generate a unique ClientId to identify the client. However, this behavior depends on the value specified for the CleanSession field.

- `CleanSession`: The clean session flag is a Boolean value that specifies what happens after an MQTT client disconnects from the MQTT server and then reconnects. If `CleanSession` is set to `1` or `True`, the client indicates to the MQTT server that the session will only last as long as the network connection is alive. After the MQTT client disconnects from the MQTT server, any information related to the session is discarded. A new connection from the same MQTT client to the MQTT server will not use the data from the previous session and will be a new clean session. If `CleanSession` is set to `0` or `False`, we will work with a persistent session. In this case, the MQTT server stores all the subscriptions for the MQTT client and when the MQTT client disconnects, the MQTT server stores all the messages that arrive with specific quality of service levels that match the subscriptions that the MQTT client had at the time the disconnection occurred. This way, when the same MQTT client establishes a new connection with the MQTT server, the MQTT client will have the same subscriptions and will receive all the messages that it couldn't receive when it lost the connection. We will dive deep into quality of service levels for messages and their relationship with the clean session flag or the persistent session option later in Chapter 2, *Using Command-Line and GUI Tools to Learn How MQTT Works.*

When the clean session flag is set to `0` or `False`, the client indicates to the server that it wants a persistent session. We just have to remember a clean session is the opposite of a persistent session.

- `UserName`: If the client wants to specify a username to request authentication and authorization from the MQTT server, it must set the `UserName` flag to `1` or `True` and specify a value for the `UserName` field

- `Password`: If the client wants to specify a password to request authentication and authorization from the MQTT server, it must set the `Password` flag to `1` or `True` and specify a value for the `Password` field

We will dedicate an entire chapter to MQTT security, and therefore we just mention the fields and the flags that are included in the CONNECT control packet.

- `ProtocolLevel`: The protocol level value indicates the MQTT protocol version that the MQTT client requests the MQTT server to use. Remember, we will always work with MQTT version 3.1.1.

- KeepAlive: KeepAlive is a time interval expressed in seconds. If the value for KeepAlive is not equal to 0, the MQTT client commits to send control packets to the server within the time specified for KeepAlive. If the MQTT client doesn't have to send any control packets, it must send a PINGREQ control packet to the MQTT server, a ping request to tell the MQTT server that the client connection is alive. The MQTT server responds to the PINGREQ control packet with a PINGRESP response to the MQTT client, a ping response to tell the MQTT client that the connection with the MQTT server is alive. The connection is closed when there is an absence of any of these control packets. If the value for KeepAlive is 0, the keep-alive mechanism is turned off.

- Will, WillQoS, WillRetain, WillTopic, and WillMessage: These flags and fields allow the MQTT client to take advantage of the last will and testament feature of MQTT. If the MQTT client sets the Will flag to 1 or True, it specifies that it wants the MQTT server to store a last will message associated with the session. The WillQoS flag specifies the desired quality of service for the last will message, and the WillRetain flag indicates whether this message must be retained when it is published. If the MQTT client sets the Will flag to 1 or True, it must specify the topic for the Will message and the message in the WillTopic and WillMessage fields. If the MQTT client is disconnected or loses the connection with the MQTT server, the MQTT server will publish the message specified in the WillMessage field to the topic indicated in the WillTopic field with the chosen quality of service. We will analyze this feature in detail later.

The MQTT server will process a valid CONNECT control packet and it will respond with a CONNACK control packet. This control packet will include values for the following flags included in the header. We want to understand the meaning of these flags because we will be able to retrieve their values when we work with MQTT tools and MQTT client libraries:

- SessionPresent: If the MQTT server received a connection request with the CleanSession flag set to 1 or True, the value for the SessionPresent flag will be 0 or False because no stored session will be reused. If the CleanSession flag was set to 0 or False in the connection request, the MQTT server will work with a persistent session, and the value for the SessionPresent flag will be 1 or True if the server had a persistent session for the client from a previous connection and retrieves it. Otherwise, SessionPresent will be 0 or False. The MQTT client that wanted to work with a persistent session can use the value of this flag to determine whether it has to request subscription to the desired topics, or whether the subscriptions have been restored from the persisted session.

- `ReturnCode`: If the authorization and authentication passed and the connection was successfully established, the value for `ReturnCode` will be 0. Otherwise, the return code will be different than 0 and the network connection between the client and the server will be closed. The following table shows the possible values for `ReturnCode` with their meanings:

ReturnCode value	Description
0	The connection was accepted
1	The connection was refused because the MQTT server doesn't support the MQTT protocol version requested by the MQTT client in the CONNECT control packet
2	The connection was refused because the `ClientId` (client identifier) specified has been rejected
3	The connection was refused because the network connection was established but the MQTT service isn't available
4	The connection was refused because the username or password values are malformed
5	The connection was refused because authorization failed

Installing a Mosquitto server on Linux

Now, we will learn the necessary steps to install a Mosquitto server on the most popular operating systems: Linux, macOS, and Windows.

 It is extremely important to work with the latest available Mosquitto versions to make sure that many security vulnerabilities discovered in previous versions are addressed. For example, Mosquitto 1.4.15 addressed two important security vulnerabilities that affected versions 1.0 to 1.4.14 inclusive.

First, we will start with Linux; specifically, we will work with Ubuntu Linux. If you want to work with a different Linux distribution, you can find details about the installation procedure in the Mosquitto downloads section: `http://mosquitto.org/download`.

Follow these steps to install a Mosquitto server on Ubuntu Linux; take into account that you will require root privileges:

1. Open a Terminal window or use a secure shell to access Ubuntu and run the following command to add the Mosquitto repository:

```
sudo apt-add-repository ppa:mosquitto-dev/mosquitto-ppa
```

You will see an output similar to the next lines (the temporary filenames will be different):

```
gpg: keyring `/tmp/tmpi5yrsz7i/secring.gpg' created
gpg: keyring `/tmp/tmpi5yrsz7i/pubring.gpg' created
gpg: requesting key 262C4500 from hkp server keyserver.ubuntu.com
gpg: /tmp/tmpi5yrsz7i/trustdb.gpg: trustdb created
gpg: key 262C4500: public key "Launchpad mosquitto" imported
gpg: Total number processed: 1
gpg: imported: 1 (RSA: 1)
OK
```

2. Run the following command to update the packages with the recently added Mosquitto repository:

```
sudo apt-get update
```

You will see an output similar to the next lines. Note that the next lines show the output of an Ubuntu server running as a Windows Azure virtual machine, and therefore the output will be similar:

```
Hit:1 http://azure.archive.ubuntu.com/ubuntu xenial InRelease
Get:2 http://azure.archive.ubuntu.com/ubuntu xenial-updates
InRelease [102 kB]
Get:3 http://azure.archive.ubuntu.com/ubuntu xenial-backports
InRelease [102 kB]

...

Get:32 http://security.ubuntu.com/ubuntu xenial-security/universe
Translation-en [121 kB]
Get:33 http://security.ubuntu.com/ubuntu xenial-
security/multiverse amd64 Packages [3,208 B]
Fetched 12.8 MB in 2s (4,809 kB/s)
Reading package lists... Done
```

3. Now, run the following command to install the package for the Mosquitto server:

```
sudo apt-get install mosquitto
```

You will see an output similar to the next lines.

4. Enter Y and press *Enter* to answer the question and complete the installation process:

```
Building dependency tree
Reading state information... Done
The following additional packages will be installed:
  libev4 libuv1 libwebsockets7
The following NEW packages will be installed:
  libev4 libuv1 libwebsockets7 mosquitto
0 upgraded, 4 newly installed, 0 to remove and 29 not upgraded.
Need to get 280 kB of archives.
After this operation, 724 kB of additional disk space will be
used.
Do you want to continue? [Y/n] Y
```

5. The last lines should include a line that says Setting up mosquitto followed by the version number, as shown in the following lines:

```
Setting up libuv1:amd64 (1.8.0-1) ...
Setting up libev4 (1:4.22-1) ...
Setting up libwebsockets7:amd64 (1.7.1-1) ...
Setting up mosquitto (1.4.15-0mosquitto1~xenial1) ...
Processing triggers for libc-bin (2.23-0ubuntu10) ...
Processing triggers for systemd (229-4ubuntu21.1) ...
Processing triggers for ureadahead (0.100.0-19) ...
```

6. Now, run the following command to install the Mosquitto client packages that will allow us to run commands to publish messages to topics and subscribe to topic filters:

```
sudo apt-get install mosquitto-clients
```

You will see an output similar to the next lines.

7. Enter Y and press *Enter* to answer the question and complete the installation process:

```
Reading package lists... Done
Building dependency tree
Reading state information... Done
The following additional packages will be installed:
```

```
   libc-ares2 libmosquitto1
The following NEW packages will be installed:
   libc-ares2 libmosquitto1 mosquitto-clients
0 upgraded, 3 newly installed, 0 to remove and 29 not upgraded.
Need to get 144 kB of archives.
After this operation, 336 kB of additional disk space will be
used.
Do you want to continue? [Y/n] Y
```

The last lines should include a line that says `Setting up mosquitto-clients` followed by the version number, as shown in the following lines:

```
Setting up libmosquitto1:amd64 (1.4.15-0mosquitto1~xenial1) ...
Setting up mosquitto-clients (1.4.15-0mosquitto1~xenial1) ...
Processing triggers for libc-bin (2.23-0ubuntu10) ...
```

8. Finally, run the following command to check the status for the `mosquitto` service that was recently installed:

```
sudo service mosquitto status
```

The first lines of the output should be similar to the following lines with an `active` (`running`) status displayed. The details after `CGroup` indicate the command line that started the service. The `-c` option followed by `/etc/mosquitto/mosquitto.conf` specifies that Mosquitto is using this configuration file:

```
mosquitto.service - LSB: mosquitto MQTT v3.1 message broker
   Loaded: loaded (/etc/init.d/mosquitto; bad; vendor preset: enabled)
   Active: active (running) since Sun 2018-03-18 19:58:15 UTC; 3min 8s ago
     Docs: man:systemd-sysv-generator(8)
   CGroup: /system.slice/mosquitto.service
           └─15126 /usr/sbin/mosquitto -c /etc/mosquitto/mosquitto.conf
```

You can also run the following command to check whether the Mosquitto MQTT server is listening at the default port, `1883`:

```
netstat -an | grep 1883
```

The following lines show the results of the previous command that indicate the Mosquitto MQTT server has opened an IPv4 and an IPv6 listen socket on port `1883`:

```
tcp 0 0 0.0.0.0:1883 0.0.0.0:* LISTEN
```

```
tcp6 0 0 :::1883 :::* LISTEN
```

Installing a Mosquitto server on macOS

Follow these steps to install a Mosquitto server on macOS, known as OS X prior to macOS Sierra:

1. If you don't have Homebrew installed, open a Terminal window and run the command indicated on the Homebrew homepage, `http://brew.sh`, to install this popular package manager for macOS. The following command will do the job. However, it is convenient to check the Homebrew homepage and check all the detailed instructions that are always updated with the newest versions of macOS that become available. If you already have Homebrew installed, move to the next step:

    ```
    /usr/bin/ruby -e "$(curl -fsSL
    https://raw.githubusercontent.com/Homebrew/install/master/install)"
    ```

2. Open a Terminal window and run the following command to request Homebrew to install Mosquitto:

    ```
    brew install mosquitto
    ```

    Notice that in some cases, Homebrew might require additional software to be installed on your computer before you can install Mosquitto. If it is necessary to install additional software, such as Xcode command-line tools, Homebrew will provide you with the necessary instructions.

3. The following lines show the last messages shown in Terminal that indicate that Homebrew has installed Mosquitto and the instructions to start the MQTT server:

    ```
    ==> Installing dependencies for mosquitto: c-ares, openssl,
    libev, libuv, libevent, libwebsockets
    ==> Installing mosquitto dependency: c-ares
    ==> Caveats
    A CA file has been bootstrapped using certificates from the
    SystemRoots
    keychain. To add additional certificates (e.g. the certificates
    added in the System keychain), place .pem files in
    /usr/local/etc/openssl/certs and run
    /usr/local/opt/openssl/bin/c_rehash

    This formula is keg-only, which means it was not symlinked into
    /usr/local, because Apple has deprecated use of OpenSSL in favor
    of its own TLS and crypto libraries. If you need to have this
    software first in your PATH run:
    ```

```
echo 'export PATH="/usr/local/opt/openssl/bin:$PATH"' >>
~/.bash_profile

For compilers to find this software you may need to set:
LDFLAGS: -L/usr/local/opt/openssl/lib
CPPFLAGS: -I/usr/local/opt/openssl/include

==> Installing mosquitto
==> Downloading https://homebrew.bintray.com/bottles/mosquitto-
    1.4.14_2.el_capit
 ###################################################
 ####################100.0%
==> Pouring mosquitto~1.4.14_2.el_capitan.bottle.tar.gz
==> Caveats
mosquitto has been installed with a default configuration file.
You can make changes to the configuration by editing:
      /usr/local/etc/mosquitto/mosquitto.conf

To have launchd start mosquitto now and restart at login:
  brew services start mosquitto

Or, if you don't want/need a background service you can just run:
  mosquitto -c /usr/local/etc/mosquitto/mosquitto.conf
```

4. After the Mosquitto installation has been completed, run the following command in a new Terminal window to launch Mosquitto with the default configuration file. The `-c` option followed by `/usr/local/etc/mosquitto/mosquitto.conf` specifies that we want to use this configuration file:

```
/usr/local/sbin/mosquitto -c
/usr/local/etc/mosquitto/mosquitto.conf
```

The following is the output after you run the previous command:

```
1521488973: mosquitto version 1.4.14 (build date 2017-10-22
16:34:20+0100) starting
1521488973: Config loaded from
/usr/local/etc/mosquitto/mosquitto.conf.
1521488973: Opening ipv4 listen socket on port 1883.
1521488973: Opening ipv6 listen socket on port 1883.
```

The last lines indicate the Mosquitto MQTT server has opened an IPv4 and an IPv6 listen socket on the default TCP port, 1883. Leave the Terminal window opened, because we need Mosquitto running on the local computer to work with the next examples.

Installing a Mosquitto server on Windows

Follow these steps to install a Mosquitto server on Windows. Take into account that you will require Windows Vista or higher (Windows 7, 8, 8.1, 10, or greater). The instructions also work on Windows Server 2008, 2012, 2016, or greater:

1. Download the executable file listed under Binary Installation and Windows that provides the native build on the Mosquitto downloads web page: `http://mosquitto.org/download`. For Mosquitto 1.4.15, the filename is `mosquitto-1.4.15-install-win32.exe`. You must click or tap on the filename and you will be redirected to the Eclipse repository with many mirror options, including a default recommendation, from which you can download the executable file.

2. Run the previously downloaded executable file and the **mosquitto Setup** Wizard will display its welcome dialog box. Click **Next >** to continue. The setup wizard will display the dependencies that you must install: OpenSSL and pthreads. The dialog box will display the links that you can use to download and run installers for these two requirements, as shown in the following screenshot:

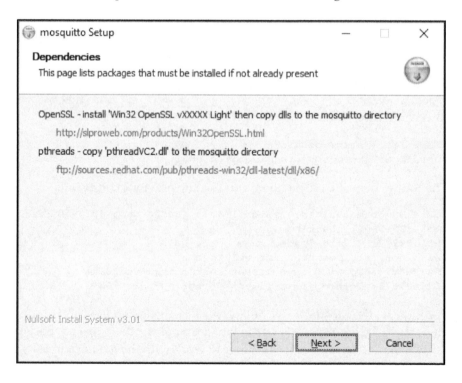

3. If you don't have Win32 OpenSSL v1.0.2j Light installed on Windows, go to the Win32 OpenSSL web page, `http://slproweb.com/products/Win32OpenSSL.html`, and download the `Win32 OpenSSL v1.1.0g Light` file listed in a table under **Download Win32 OpenSSL**. Do not download the Win64 version, because you will need the Win32 version to make it possible for Mosquitto to have its dependencies. If you already have Win32 OpenSSL v1.1.0g Light installed, advance to step 7. For Win32 OpenSSL v1.1.0g Light, the filename is `Win32OpenSSL_Light-1_1_0g.exe`. Run the downloaded executable file and OpenSSL Light (32-bit) will display its welcome dialog box. Click **Next >** to continue.

4. The setup wizard will display the License Agreement. Read it, select **I Accept the agreement**, and click **Next >**. Select the folder in which you want to install OpenSSL Light (32-bit) if you don't want to use the default folder. Remember the folder you specify, because you will need to copy a few DLL files from this folder later. The default folder is `C:\OpenSSL-Win32`.

5. Click **Next >** to continue, specify a different Start Menu folder if necessary, and click **Next >**. Select **The OpenSSL binaries (/bin) directory** as the desired option for **Copy OpenSSL DLLs to**. This way, the installation will copy the DLLs to a `bin` subfolder within the previously specified folder, by default `C:\OpenSSL-Win32\bin`.

6. Click **Next >** to continue. Review the selected installation options and click **Install** to complete the installation for OpenSSL Light (32-bit). Finally, consider a donation to the Win32 OpenSSL project and click **Finish** to exit setup.

7. Go to the following address in your web browser: `ftp://sources.redhat.com/pub/pthreads-win32/dll-latest/dll/x86`. The browser will display many files for this FTP directory. Right-click on **pthreadVC2.dll** and save the file in your `Downloads` folder. You will have to copy this DLL to the Mosquitto installation folder later.

8. Now, go back to the **mosquitto Setup** window and click **Next >** to continue. By default, Mosquitto will install the files and the Mosquitto Service. Leave the default components to install those selected and click **Next >** to continue.

9. Select the folder in which you want to install Mosquitto if you don't want to use the default folder. Remember the folder you specify, because you will need to copy a few DLL files to this folder later. The default folder is `C:\Program Files (x86)\mosquitto`. Click **Install** to complete the installation. Notice that the **mosquitto Setup** Wizard might display errors related to missing DLLs. We will fix this issue in the next steps. Once the installation has completed, click **Finish** to close the **mosquitto Setup** Wizard.

10. Open a **File Explorer** window and go to the bin subfolder within the folder in which you installed OpenSSL Light (32-bit), by default C:\OpenSSL-Win32\bin.

11. Copy the following four DLLs: libcrypto-1_1.dll, libeay32.dll, ssleay32.dll, and libssl-1_1.dll. Now, go to the folder in which you installed Mosquitto and paste these four DLLs. By default, the Mosquitto installation folder is C:\Program Files (x86)\mosquitto. You will need to provide administrator permission to paste the DLLs in the default folder.

12. Open a **File Explorer** window and go to your Downloads folder. Copy the pthreads DLL you downloaded in one of the previous steps, pthreadVC2.dll. Now, go to the folder in which you installed Mosquitto and paste this DLL. You will need to provide administrator permission to paste the DLL into the default Mosquitto installation folder.

13. Now that all the dependencies are included in the Mosquitto installation folder, it is necessary to run the installation again to make the Mosquitto setup configure the Windows service. Run the previously downloaded Mosquitto installation executable again. For Mosquitto 1.4.15, the filename is mosquito-1.4.15-install-win32.exe. Make sure you specify the same installation folder as the folder in which you copied the DLLs and that the Service component is activated. Click **Next >** many times and click **Install** to complete the configuration for the Windows service. Once the installation has completed, click Finish to close the **mosquitto Setup** Wizard.

14. Open the **Services** application in Windows and search for the service whose name is **Mosquitto Broker**. Right-click on the service name and select **Start**. The Status will change to **Running**. By default, the service is configured to have its **Startup Type** set to **Automatic**. If you don't want to automatically start the **Mosquitto Broker** service, change the **Startup Type** to **Manual**. You will have to repeat the step you just did to manually start the service before working with Mosquitto on a Windows computer. Notice that the description for the service is **MQTT v3.1 broker**, as shown in the following screenshot. The description is outdated because the service provides an MQTT 3.1.1 server that is also compatible with MQTT 3.1:

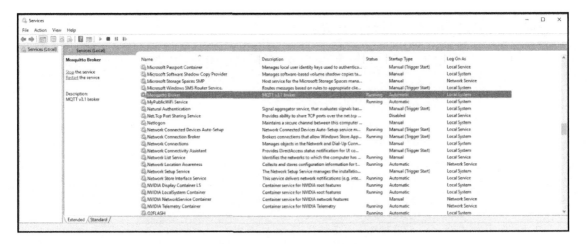

Open a Windows PowerShell or a Command Prompt window and run the following command to check whether the Mosquitto MQTT server is listening at the default TCP port, 1883:

```
netstat -an | findstr 1883
```

The following lines show the results of the previous command that indicate the Mosquitto MQTT server has opened an IPv4 and an IPv6 listen socket on port 1883:

```
TCP 0.0.0.0:1883 0.0.0.0:0 LISTENING
TCP [::]:1883 [::]:0 LISTENING
```

Considerations for running a Mosquitto server in the cloud

We have worked with the default configuration for a Mosquitto server in Linux, macOS, and Windows. The Mosquitto server will work with TCP port 1883. If you want to interact with the Mosquitto server from a different device or computer, you have to make sure that the firewall that is running on your computer has the appropriate configuration for this port number.

When you run a Mosquitto server on a Linux or Windows virtual machine in the cloud, you also have to make sure that the virtual machine network filter that controls both inbound and outbound traffic has the appropriate configuration to allow inbound and outbound traffic on port 1883. You must authorize inbound and outbound traffic on port 1883.

Test your knowledge

Let's see whether you can answer the following questions correctly:

1. MQTT runs on top of:
    1. The MQIP protocol
    2. The TCP/IP protocol
    3. The IoT protocol

2. The data for an MQTT message is known as:
    1. Payload
    2. Packet
    3. Upload

3. In MQTT version 3.1.1, the broker is named:
    1. MQTT agent
    2. MQTT client
    3. MQTT server

4. Mosquitto is:
    1. A cloud-based MQTT server that is only available on Windows Azure
    2. A cloud-based MQTT server that is only available on Amazon Web Services
    3. An open source MQTT server compatible with MQTT versions 3.1.1 and 3.1

5. The default TCP port that a Mosquitto server uses is:
    1. 22
    2. 1883
    3. 9000

The rights answers are included in the `Appendix`, *Solutions*.

Summary

In this chapter, we started our journey toward understanding the MQTT protocol. We understood convenient scenarios for this protocol, the details of the publish-subscribe pattern, and message filtering. We learned basic concepts related to MQTT and understood the different components: clients, servers or brokers, and connections.

We learned to install a Mosquitto server on Linux, macOS, and Windows. We used the default configuration, as it allowed us to learn how everything works under the hood while using Mosquitto. Then, we will secure the server. This way, it will be easier for us to start using the client libraries in Python to publish MQTT messages and subscribe to MQTT topic filters.

Now that we have our environment ready to start working with a still-unsecured Mosquitto server, we will work with command-line and GUI tools to learn how MQTT works in detail. We will learn MQTT basics, the specific vocabulary for MQTT, and its working modes, which are the topics that we are going to discuss in Chapter 2, *Using Command-Line and GUI Tools to Learn How MQTT Works*.

2
Using Command-Line and GUI Tools to Learn How MQTT Works

In this chapter, we will work with command-line and GUI tools to learn how MQTT 3.1.1 works in detail. We will learn MQTT basics, the specific vocabulary for MQTT, and its working modes. We will use different utilities and diagrams to understand the most important concepts related to MQTT. We will understand everything we need to know before writing Python code to work with the MQTT protocol. We will work with the different Quality of Service (QoS) levels and we will analyze and compare their overheads. We will gain an understanding of the following:

- Subscribing to topics with a command-line tool
- Subscribing to topics with a GUI tool
- Publishing messages with a command-line tool
- Publishing messages with a GUI tool
- Unsubscribing from topics with a GUI tool
- Learning best practices for topics
- Understanding MQTT wildcards
- Learning about the different quality of service levels
- Working with at least once delivery (QoS level 1)
- Working with exactly once delivery (QoS level 2)
- Understanding overheads in the different quality of service levels

Subscribing to topics with a command-line tool

A drone is an IoT device that interacts with many sensors and actuators, including digital electronic speed controllers linked to engines, propellers, and servomotors. A drone is also known as an **unmanned aerial vehicle (UAV)**, but we will definitely refer to it as a drone. Let's imagine that we have to monitor many drones. Specifically, we have to display their altitude and the speed for each of their servomotors. Not all of the drones have the same number of engines, propellers, and servomotors. We have to monitor the following types of drone:

Name	Number of propellers
Quadcopter	4
Hexacopter	6
Octocopter	8

Each drone will publish its altitude every 2 seconds to the following topic: `sensors/dronename/altitude`, where `dronename` must be replaced by the name assigned to each drone. For example, the drone named `octocopter01` will publish its altitude values to the `sensors/octocopter01/altitude` topic and the drone named `quadcopter20` will use the `sensors/quadcopter20/altitude` topic.

In addition, each drone will publish the speed for each of its rotors every 2 seconds to the following topic: `sensors/dronename/speed/rotor/rotornumber`, where `dronename` must be replaced by the name assigned to each drone and `rotornumber` must be replaced by the rotor number for which the speed is going to be published. For example, the drone named `octocopter01` will publish its speed values for its rotor number 1 to the `sensors/octocopter01/speed/rotor/1` topic.

We will use the `mosquitto_sub` command-line utility included in Mosquitto to generate a simple MQTT client that subscribes to a topic and prints all the messages it receives. Open a Terminal in macOS or Linux, or a Command Prompt in Windows, go to the directory in which Mosquitto is installed, and run the following command:

```
mosquitto_sub -V mqttv311 -t sensors/octocopter01/altitude -d
```

If you want to work with Windows PowerShell instead of the Command Prompt, you will have to add `.\` as a prefix to `mosquitto_sub`.

The previous command will create an MQTT client that will establish a connection with the local MQTT server and then will make the client subscribe to the topic specified after the `-t` option: `sensors/octocopter01/altitude`. We specify the version of the MQTT protocol that we want to use when the client establishes the connection with `-V mqttv311`. This way, we indicate to the MQTT server that we want to use MQTT version 3.11. We specify the `-d` option to enable debug messages that will allow us to understand what happens under the hood. We will analyze additional options for connection and subscription later.

The Terminal or Command Prompt window will display debug messages similar to the following lines. Take into account that the generated `ClientId` will be different from the one shown after `Client mosqsub|17040-LAPTOP-5D`:

```
Client mosqsub|17040-LAPTOP-5D sending CONNECT
Client mosqsub|17040-LAPTOP-5D received CONNACK
Client mosqsub|17040-LAPTOP-5D sending SUBSCRIBE (Mid: 1, Topic:
sensors/octocopter01/altitude, QoS: 0)
Client mosqsub|17040-LAPTOP-5D received SUBACK
Subscribed (mid: 1): 0
```

The Terminal or Command Prompt window will display messages published to the topic to which we subscribed as they arrive from the MQTT server to the MQTT client. Keep the window open. You will see that that the client sends `PINGREQ` packets to the MQTT server and receives `PINQRESP` packets from the MQTT server. The following lines show examples of the messages displayed for these packets:

```
Client mosqsub|17040-LAPTOP-5D sending PINGREQ
Client mosqsub|17040-LAPTOP-5D received PINGRESP
```

Subscribing to topics with a GUI tool

MQTT.fx is a GUI utility implemented with JavaFX that is available for Windows, Linux, and macOS. This tool allows us to connect with an MQTT server, subscribe to topic filters, see received messages, and publish messages to topics. You can download the appropriate version for your operating system from the downloads section of the main web page for this utility: `http://www.mqttfx.org`.

Now, we will use the MQTT.fx GUI utility to generate another MQTT client that subscribes to the same topic, `sensors/octocopter01/altitude`, and displays all the messages it receives. We will work with MQTT.fx version 1.6.0. Follow these steps:

1. Launch MQTT.fx, select **local mosquitto** in the dropdown located at the upper-left corner, and click on the configuration icon at the right-hand side of this dropdown and at the left-hand side of the **Connect** button. MQTT.fx will display the **Edit Connection Profiles** dialog box with different options for the connection profile named **local mosquitto**. We analyzed many of these options when we learned about the data that the MQTT client sends to the MQTT server to establish a connection.

2. Make sure the **General** button is pressed and make sure the **MQTT Version Use Default** checkbox is deactivated. Make sure 3.1.1 is selected in the dropdown below **MQTT Version**. This way, we tell the MQTT server that we want to use MQTT version 3.11. Notice that the **Client ID** textbox specifies **MQTT_FX_Client**. This is the `ClientId` value that MQTT.fx will send to the MQTT server (Mosquitto) in the `CONNECT` control packet. The following screenshot shows a dialog box with the selected options:

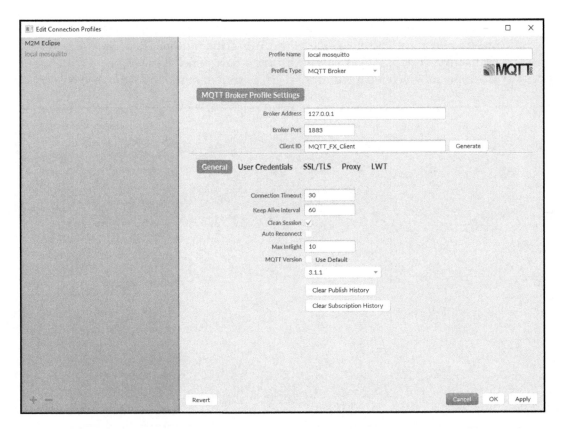

3. Click **OK** and then click on the **Connect** button. MQTT.fx will establish a connection with the local Mosquitto server. Notice that the **Connect** button is disabled and the **Disconnect** button is enabled because the client is connected to the MQTT server.

4. Click **Subscribe** and enter `sensors/octocopter01/altitude` in the dropdown at the left-hand side of the **Subscribe** button. Then, click the **Subscribe** button. MQTT.fx will display a new panel at the left-hand side with the topic to which we have subscribed, as shown in the following screenshot:

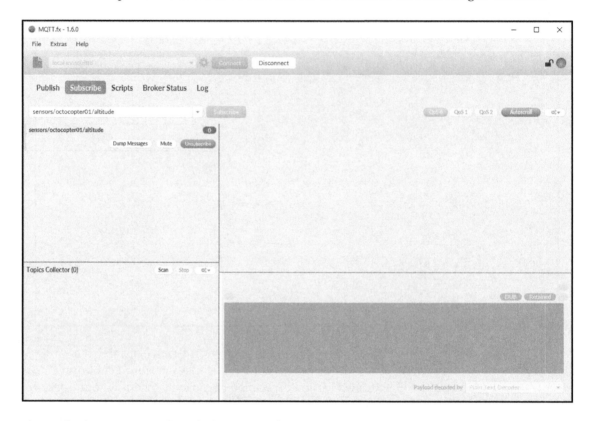

If you don't want to work with the MQTT.fx utility, you can run another `mosquitto_sub` command to generate another MQTT client that subscribes to the topic and print all the messages it receives. You just need to open another Terminal in macOS or Linux, or another Command Prompt in Windows, go to the directory in which Mosquitto is installed, and run the following command again. In this case, it isn't necessary to specify the `-d` option as given here:

```
mosquitto_sub -V mqttv311 -t sensors/octocopter01/altitude
```

Now, we have two MQTT clients subscribed to the same topic: `sensors/octocopter01/altitude`. Now, we will understand what happens under the hood when a client subscribes to a topic.

The MQTT client sends a SUBSCRIBE packet to the MQTT server with a packet identifier (PacketId) in the header and one or more topic filters with their desired quality of service level in the payload.

 Quality of service is known as **QoS**.

Hence, a single SUBSCRIBE packet can ask the MQTT server to subscribe a client to many topics. The SUBSCRIBE packet must include at least one topic filter and a QoS pair to comply with the protocol.

In the two cases in which we requested a subscription, we used a specific topic name as the value for the topic filter, and therefore we request the MQTT server to subscribe to a single topic. We will learn about the use of wildcards in topic filters later.

We used the default options, and therefore the quality of service requested is the default level of 0. We will dive deep into QoS levels later. Now, we will stay focused on the simplest subscription cases. If the QoS level is equal to 0, the value for the PacketId field will be 0. If the QoS level is equal to 1 or 2, the packet identifier will have a number value to identify the packet and make it possible to identify the responses related to this packet.

The MQTT server will process a valid SUBSCRIBE packet and it will respond with a SUBACK packet that indicates the subscribe acknowledgment and confirms the receipt and processing of the SUBSCRIBE packet. The SUBACK packet will include the same packet identifier (PacketId) in the header that was received in the SUBSCRIBE packet. The SUBACK packet will include one return code for each pair of a topic filter and the desired QoS level received in the SUBSCRIBE packet. The number of return codes will match the number of topic filters included in the SUBSCRIBE packet. The following table shows the possible values for these return codes. The first three return codes indicate a successful subscription and each value specifies the maximum QoS that can be delivered based on the requested QoS and the possibilities that the MQTT server has to grant the requested QoS:

ReturnCode value	Description
0	Successfully subscribed with a maximum QoS of 0
1	Successfully subscribed with a maximum QoS of 1
2	Successfully subscribed with a maximum QoS of 2
128	Failed to subscribe

If the subscription was successful, the MQTT server will start sending every published message that matches the topic filters specified in the subscription to the MQTT client with the QoS specified in the return code.

The following diagram shows the interaction between an MQTT client and an MQTT server to subscribe to one or many topic filters:

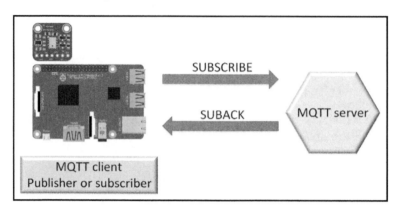

Publishing messages with a command-line tool

We will use the mosquitto_pub command-line utility included in Mosquitto to generate a simple MQTT client that publishes a message to a topic. Open a Terminal in macOS or Linux, or a Command Prompt in Windows, go to the directory in which Mosquitto is installed, and run the following command:

```
mosquitto_pub -V mqttv311 -t sensors/octocopter01/altitude -m  "25 f" -d
```

The previous command will create an MQTT client that will establish a connection with the local MQTT server and then will make the client publish a message to the topic specified after the -t option: sensors/octocopter01/altitude. We specify the payload for the message after the -m option: "25 f". We specify the version of the MQTT protocol that we want to use when the client establishes the connection with -V mqttv311. This way, we indicate to the MQTT server that we want to use MQTT version 3.11. We specify the -d option to enable debug messages that will allow us to understand what happens under the hood. We will analyze additional options for connection and publication later.

The Terminal or Command Prompt window will display debug messages similar to the following lines. Take into account that the generated `ClientId` will be different from the one shown after `Client mosqpub|17912-LAPTOP-5D`. After publishing the message, the client disconnects:

```
Client mosqpub|17912-LAPTOP-5D sending CONNECT
Client mosqpub|17912-LAPTOP-5D received CONNACK
Client mosqpub|17912-LAPTOP-5D sending PUBLISH (d0, q0, r0, m1,
'sensors/octocopter01/altitude', ... (4 bytes))
Client mosqpub|17912-LAPTOP-5D sending DISCONNECT
```

Publishing messages with a GUI tool

Now, we will use the MQTT.fx GUI utility to generate another MQTT client that publishes another message to the same topic, sensors/octocopter01/altitude. Follow these steps:

1. Go to the MQTT.fx window in which you established a connection and subscribed to a topic.
2. Click **Publish** and enter `sensors/octocopter01/altitude` in the dropdown at the left-hand side of the **Publish** button.
3. Enter the following text in the textbox below the **Publish** button: `32 f`, as shown in the following screenshot:

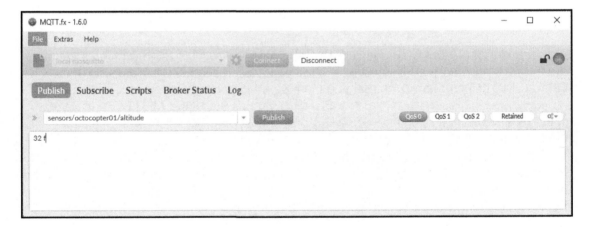

4. Then, click the **Publish** button. MQTT.fx will publish the entered text to the specified topic.

If you don't want to work with the MQTT.fx utility, you can run another `mosquitto_pub` command to generate another MQTT client that publishes a message to the topic. You just need to open another Terminal in macOS or Linux, or another Command Prompt in Windows, go to the directory in which Mosquitto is installed, and run the following command:

```
mosquitto_pub -V mqttv311 -t sensors/octocopter01/altitude -m "32 f"
```

Now, go back to the Terminal or Command Prompt window in which you executed the `mosquitto_sub` command and subscribed to the `sensors/octocopter01/atitude` topic. You will see lines similar to the following ones:

```
Client mosqsub|3476-LAPTOP-5DO received PUBLISH (d0, q0, r0, m0,
'sensors/octocopter01/altitude', ... (4 bytes))
25 f
Client mosqsub|3476-LAPTOP-5DO received PUBLISH (d0, q0, r0, m0,
'sensors/octocopter01/altitude', ... (4 bytes))
32 f
```

If we clean up debug messages that start with the **Client** prefix, we will see just the next two lines. These lines show the payloads for the two messages that we received as a result of our subscription to the `sensors/octocopter01/altitude` topic:

```
25 f
32 f
```

Go to the MQTT.fx window and click **Subscribe**. You will see **2** at the right-hand side of the title for the topic filter used to subscribe in the panel located at the left-hand side of the window. MQTT.fx is telling you that you have received two messages in the `sensors/octocopter01/altitude` topic. Click on this panel and MQTT.fx will display all the received messages on the right-hand side of the panel. MQTT.fx will display a number at the right-hand side of each message to specify the message number since we started the subscription to the topic filter. Click on each message and MQTT.fx will display the QoS level for the message (0), the date and time it was received, and the payload for the message in the default plain string format. The following screenshot shows the payload for the second message that has been received by the subscriber generated by MQTT.fx:

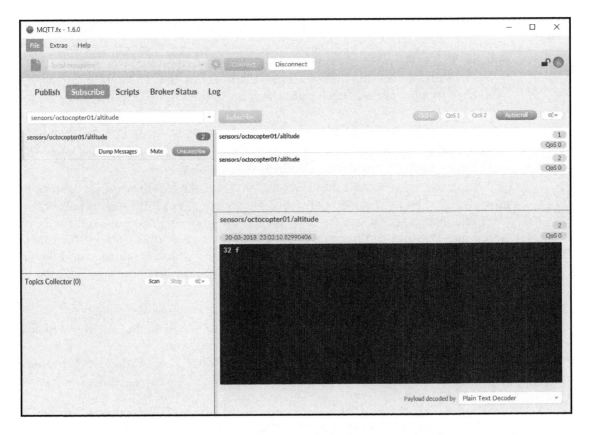

We created two publishers and each of them published a message to the same topic: `sensors/octocopter01/altitude`. The two subscribers for this topic received both messages. Now, we will understand what happens under the hood when a client publishes a message to a topic.

The MQTT client that has already established a connection sends a `PUBLISH` packet to the MQTT server with a header that includes the following fields and flags. We need to understand the meaning of these fields and flags because we will be able to specify some of their values when we work with MQTT tools and MQTT client libraries in Python:

- `PacketId`: If the QoS level is equal to 0, the value for this field will be 0 or it won't be present. If the QoS level is equal to 1 or 2, the packet identifier will have a number value to identify the packet and make it possible to identify the responses related to this packet.

- `Dup`: If the QoS level is equal to 0, the value for this field will be 0. If the QoS level is equal to 1 or 2, the MQTT client library or the MQTT server can resend a message that was previously published by the client when the subscribers haven't acknowledged the first message. Whenever there is an attempt to resend a message that has already been published, the value for the Dup flag must be 1 or `True`.

- `QoS`: Specifies the QoS level for the message. We will dive deep into the quality of service level for messages, and their relationship with many other flags, later. So far, we have been working with QoS level 0.

- `Retain`: If the value for this flag is set to 1 or `True`, the MQTT server will store the message with its specified QoS level. Whenever new MQTT clients subscribe to a topic filter that matches the topic for the stored or retained message, the last stored message for this topic will be sent to the new subscriber. If the value for this flag is set to 0 or `False`, the MQTT server won't store the message and won't replace a retained message with the same topic if there is one message retained for this topic.

- `TopicName`: A string with the topic name to which the message must be published. Topic names have a hierarchy structure where slashes (/) are used as delimiters. In our examples, the value for `TopicName` was `"sensors/octocopter01/altitude"`. We will analyze best practices for topic names later.

The payload contains the actual message that the MQTT client wants the MQTT server to publish. MQTT is data-agnostic, and therefore we can send any binary data and we don't have restrictions such as those imposed by JSON or XML. Of course, we can use these or others to organize payloads if we wish. In our examples, we sent a string that included a number that represented the altitude, followed by a space, and an `"f"` that indicates the unit of measurement is `feet`.

The MQTT server will read a valid `PUBLISH` packet and it will respond with a packet only for QoS levels greater than 0. If the QoS level is 0, the MQTT server will not respond. The MQTT server will identify all subscribers whose subscribed topic matches the topic name specified for the message and the server will publish the message to these clients.

The following diagram shows the interaction between an MQTT client and an MQTT server to publish a message with a QoS level of 0:

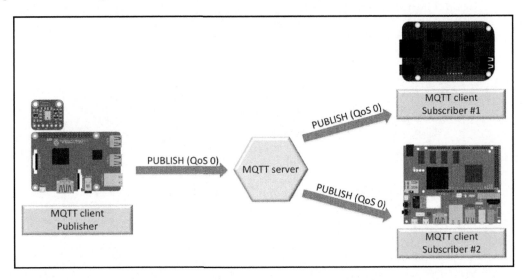

The other QoS levels have a different flow with an additional interaction between the publisher and the MQTT server, and increased overheads that we will analyze later.

Unsubscribing from topics with a GUI tool

Whenever we don't want a subscriber to receive more messages whose destination topic name matches one or more topic filters, the subscriber can send a request to unsubscribe to a list of topic filters to the MQTT server. Obviously, unsubscribing from topic filters is the opposite of subscribing to topic filters. We will use the MQTT.fx GUI utility to unsubscribe the MQTT client from the `sensors/octocopter01/altitude` topic. Follow these steps:

1. Go to the MQTT.fx window in which you established a connection and subscribed to a topic.
2. Click **Subscribe**.

3. Click on the panel that displays the `sensors/octocopter01/altitude` topic name on the left-hand side of the window. Then, click on the **Unsubscribe** button located in this panel. The following screenshot shows this button:

4. MQTT.fx will unsubscribe the client from the `sensors/octocopter01/altitude` topic, and therefore the client won't receive any new messages published to the `sensors/octocopter01/altitude` topic.

Now, we will use the MQTT.fx GUI utility to make the MQTT client publish another message to the `sensors/octocopter01/altitude`. Follow these steps:

1. Go to the MQTT.fx window in which you established a connection and subscribed to a topic.
2. Click **Publish** and enter `sensors/octocopter01/altitude` in the dropdown at the left-hand side of the **Publish** button.
3. Then, click the **Publish** button. MQTT.fx will publish the entered text to the specified topic.

4. Enter the following text in the textbox below the **Publish** button: 37 f, as shown in the following screenshot:

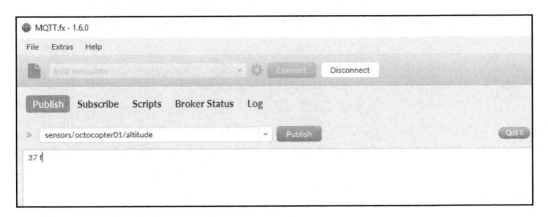

If you don't want to work with the MQTT.fx utility, you can run a mosquitto_pub command to generate another MQTT client that publishes a message to the topic. You just need to open another Terminal in macOS or Linux, or another Command Prompt in Windows, go to the directory in which Mosquitto is installed, and run the following command:

```
mosquitto_pub -V mqttv311 -t sensors/octocopter01/altitude -m "37 f"
```

Now, go back to the MQTT.fx window and click **Subscribe** to check the messages that have been received. The client has unsubscribed from the sensors/octocopter01/altitude topic before we published a new message to this topic, and therefore the recently published message with a payload of "37 f" isn't displayed.

Go back to the Terminal or Command Prompt window in which you executed the mosquitto_sub command and subscribed to the sensors/octocopter01/atitude topic. You will see lines similar to the following:

```
Client mosqsub|3476-LAPTOP-5DO received PUBLISH (d0, q0, r0, m0,
'sensors/octocopter01/altitude', ... (4 bytes))
37 f
```

This client is still subscribed to the sensors/octocopter01/altitude topic, and therefore it received the message with the payload of "37 f".

The MQTT client sends an UNSUBSCRIBE packet to the MQTT server with a packet identifier (PacketId) in the header and one or more topic filters in the payload. The main difference with a SUBSCRIBE packet is that it isn't necessary to include the QoS level for each topic filter because the MQTT client just wants to unsubscribe.

> After an MQTT client unsubscribes from one or more topic filters, the MQTT server still keeps the connection open; the subscriptions to topic filters that don't match the topic filters specified in the UNSUBSCRIBE packet payload will continue working.

Hence, a single UNSUBSCRIBE packet can ask the MQTT server to unsubscribe a client from many topics. The UNSUBSCRIBE packet must include at least one topic filter in the payload to comply with the protocol.

In the previous example, in which we asked the MQTT server to unsubscribe, we used a specific topic name as the value for the topic filter, and therefore we requested the MQTT server to unsubscribe from a single topic. As previously mentioned, we will learn about the use of wildcards in topic filters later.

The packet identifier will have a number value to identify the packet and make it possible to identify the response related to this UNSUBSCRIBE packet. The MQTT server will process a valid UNSUBSCRIBE packet and it will respond with an UNSUBACK packet, which indicates the unsubscribe acknowledgment and confirms the receipt and processing of the UNSUBSCRIBE packet. The UNSUBACK packet will include the same packet identifier (PacketId) in the header that was received in the UNSUBSCRIBE packet.

The MQTT server will remove any topic filter that exactly matches any of the specified topic filters in the UNSUBSCRIBE packet's payload for the specific client that sent the packet. The topic filter match must be exact to be deleted. After the MQTT server deletes a topic filter from the subscription list for the client, the server stops adding new messages to be published to the client. Only messages that have already started delivery to the client with QoS levels of 1 or 2 will be published to the client. In addition, the server might publish existing messages that have been buffered for their distribution to the subscriber.

The following diagram shows the interaction between an MQTT client and an MQTT server in unsubscribing from one or many topic filters:

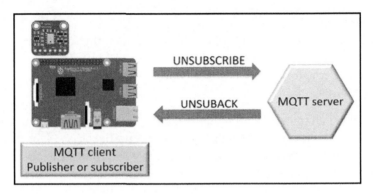

Learning best practices for topics

We already know that MQTT allows us to publish messages on topics. A publisher always has to specify the topic name to which a message will be published. The easiest way to understand topic names in MQTT is to think about them as paths in a file system.

If we have to save dozens of files that have information about different types of sensor for a diverse number of drones, we can create a hierarchy of directories or folders to organize all the files that we will save. We can create a directory named sensors, then one sub-directory for each drone, such as octocopter01, and finally a sub-directory with the sensor name, such as altitude. The path in macOS or Linux will be sensors/octocopter01/altitude because these operating systems use a forward slash (/) as a delimiter. In Windows, the path will be sensors\drone\altitude because this operating system uses a backslash (\) as a delimiter.

Then, we will save the files that have information about the altitude sensor for the drone named octocopter01 in the created path. Instead of saving files in a path, we can think about publishing a message to a path and using the same mechanism we use to organize files in paths to arrange messages in topics.

Instead of directories or folders, a topic has topic levels, specifically a hierarchy of topic levels, and slashes (/) are used as delimiters, that is, topic-level separators. If we use sensors/octocopter01/altitude as the topic name, sensors is the first topic level, octocopter01 is the second topic level, and altitude is the third topic level.

Topic names are case-sensitive, and therefore `sensors/octocopter01/altitude` is different from `sensors/Octocopter01/altitude`, `Sensors/octocopter01/altitude`, and `Sensors/Octocopter01/Altitude`. In fact, the four strings will be considered as four individual topic names. We must make sure we select a case scheme for the topic names and we use it for all topic names and topic filters.

We can use any UTF-8 character in topic names, with the exception of the two wildcard characters that we will analyze later: the plus sign (+) and hash (#). Hence, we must avoid + and # in the topic names. However, it is a good practice to restrict the character set to avoid unexpected problems with client libraries. For example, we can avoid accents and characters that are not common in English, as we do whenever we build URLs. It is possible to use these characters but you can definitely face issues when using them.

We should avoid creating topics starting with the dollar sign ($) because many MQTT servers publish statistics data related to servers in topics that start with $. Specifically, the first topic level is `$SYS`.

We must maintain consistency when sending messages to different topic names as we do when we save files in different paths. For example, if we want to publish the altitude for a drone named `hexacopter20`, we will use `sensors/hexacopter20/altitude`. We must use the same topic levels that we used for the same goal for `octocopter01` and just change the drone name from `octocopter01` to `hexacopter20`. It would be a really bad practice to use a topic with a different structure or an inconsistent case, such as `altitude/sensors/hexacopter20` or `Sensors/Hexacopter20/Altitude`. We have to take into account that we can subscribe to multiple topics by using topic filters, and therefore it is very important to create topic names accordingly.

Understanding MQTT wildcards

When we analyzed the subscription operation, we learned that an MQTT client can subscribe to one or more topic filters. If we specify a topic name as a topic filter, we will only subscribe to a single topic. We can take advantage of the following two wildcards to create topic filters that subscribe to all the topics that match the filter:

- **Plus sign** (+): This is a single-level wildcard that matches any name for a specific topic level. We can use this wildcard instead of specifying a name for any topic level in the topic filter.

- **Hash** (#): This is a multilevel wildcard that we can use only at the end of a topic filter, as the last level, and it matches any topic whose first levels are the same as the topic levels specified at the left-hand side of the # symbol.

For example, if we want to receive all the messages related to altitude for all the drones, we can use the + single-level wildcard instead of a specific drone name. We can use the following topic filter: `sensors/+/altitude`.

If we publish messages to the following topics, the subscriber that used the `sensors/+/altitude` topic filter will receive all of them:

- `sensors/octocopter01/altitude`
- `sensors/hexacopter20/altitude`
- `sensors/superdrone01/altitude`
- `sensors/thegreatestdrone/altitude`

The subscriber to the `sensors/+/altitude` topic filter won't receive messages sent to any of the following topics because they won't match the topic filter:

- `sensors/octocopter01/speed/rotor/1`
- `sensors/superdrone01/speed/rotor/2`
- `sensors/superdrone01/remainingbattery`

If we want to receive all the messages related to all the sensors for the drone named `octocopter01`, we can use the # multilevel wildcard after the drone name and the slash (/). We can use the following topic filter: `sensors/octocopter01/#`.

If we publish messages to the following topics, the subscriber that used the `sensors/octocopter01/#` topic filter will receive all of them:

- `sensors/octocopter01/altitude`
- `sensors/octocopter01/speed/rotor/1`
- `sensors/octocopter01/speed/rotor/2`
- `sensors/octocopter01/speed/rotor/3`
- `sensors/octocopter01/speed/rotor/4`
- `sensors/octocopter01/remainingbattery`

We used a multilevel wildcard, and therefore, irrespective of the additional topic levels after `sensors/octocopter01/`, we will receive all of them.

The subscriber to the `sensors/octocopter01/#` topic filter won't receive messages sent to any of the following topics because they won't match the topic filter. None of the following has `sensors/octocopter01/` as a prefix, and therefore they don't match the topic filter:

- `sensors/hexacopter02/altitude`
- `sensors/superdrone01/altitude`
- `sensors/thegreatestdrone/altitude`
- `sensors/drone02/speed/rotor/1`
- `sensors/superdrone02/speed/rotor/2`
- `sensors/superdrone02/remainingbattery`

Obviously, we must be careful when we use any wildcard because we might be subscribing to a huge number of topics with a single topic filter. We have to avoid subscribing to topics that aren't of interest for the client to avoid wasting unnecessary bandwidth and server resources.

We will use these wildcards in subscriptions later to analyze how different QoS levels work with MQTT.

Learning about the different QoS levels

Now that we understand how connection, subscription, and publication work in combination with topic names and topic filters with wildcards, we can dive deep into the QoS levels. So far, we have analyzed how both subscription and publication work with a QoS level equal to 0. Now, we will understand what this number means and how things work when we use the other available QoS levels for publication and subscription.

 Remember that publication involves publishing from the MQTT client to the MQTT server and then from the server to the subscribed client. It is very important to understand that we can publish with a QoS level and subscribe with another QoS level. Hence, there is a QoS level for the publish process between the publisher and the MQTT server and another QoS level for the publish process between the MQTT server and the subscriber. We will use sender and receiver to identify the parties involved in message delivery for the different QoS levels. In the publish process between the publisher and the MQTT server, the publisher will be the sender and the MQTT server the receiver. In the publish process between the MQTT server and the subscriber, the sender will be the MQTT server and the receiver will be the subscriber.

Based on the QoS level, we have differences in the meaning of a successfully delivered message in the MQTT protocol between the involved parties. The QoS level is the agreement between a sender and a receiver of a message about the guarantees of actually delivering the message. These warranties might include the number of times that a message might arrive and the possibility (or not) of duplicates. MQTT supports the following three possible QoS levels:

- **0, At most once delivery**: This QoS level offers the same warranty as the underlying TCP protocol. The message is not acknowledged by the receiver or destination. The sender just sends the message to the destination and nothing else happens. The sender neither stores nor schedules new deliveries for any messages that might fail to reach the destination. The key advantage of this QoS level is that it has the lowest possible overhead, compared to the other QoS levels.

- **1, At least once delivery**: This QoS level adds a confirmation requirement to the destination that has to receive the message. This way, QoS level 1 provides a warranty that the message will be delivered at least once to the subscriber. One of the key disadvantages of this QoS level is that it might generate duplicates, that is, the same message might be sent more than once to the same destination. The sender stores the message until it receives an acknowledgment from the subscriber. If the sender doesn't receive the acknowledgment within a specific time, the sender will publish the message again to the receiver. The final receiver must have the necessary logic to detect duplicates if they shouldn't be processed twice.

- **2, Exactly once delivery**: This QoS level provides a warranty that the message is delivered only once to the destination. QoS level 2 has the highest overhead, compared to the other QoS levels. This QoS level requires two flows between the sender and the receiver. A message published with QoS level 2 is considered successfully delivered after the sender is sure that it has been successfully received once by the destination.

Sometimes, we just want messages to be delivered with the least possible bandwidth usage, we have a very reliable network, and it doesn't matter if for some reason a few messages are lost. In these cases, QoS level 0 is the appropriate choice.

In other cases, the messages are extremely important because they represent commands to control an IoT device, the network is unreliable, and we must make sure that the message reaches the destination. In addition, a duplicate command might generate a big problem because we don't want the IoT device to process a specific command twice. In these cases, QoS level 2 is going to be the appropriate choice.

If a publisher works with a QoS level higher than the QoS level specified by the subscriber, the MQTT server will have to downgrade the QoS level to the lowest level that the specific subscriber is using when it publishes the message from the MQTT server to this subscriber. For example, if we use QoS level 2 to publish a message from the publisher to the MQTT server, but one subscriber has requested QoS level 1 when making the subscription, the publication from the MQTT server to this subscriber will use QoS level 1.

Working with at least once delivery (QoS level 1)

First, we will use wildcards to subscribe to a topic filter with QoS level 1, and then we will publish one message to a topic name that will match the topic filter with QoS level 1. This way, we will analyze how both publishing and subscription work with QoS level 1.

We will use the `mosquitto_sub` command-line utility included in Mosquitto to generate a simple MQTT client that subscribes to a topic filter with QoS level 1 and prints all the messages it receives. Open a Terminal in macOS or Linux, or a Command Prompt in Windows, go to the directory in which Mosquitto is installed, and run the following command:

```
mosquitto_sub -V mqttv311 -t sensors/+/altitude -q 1 -d
```

The previous command will create an MQTT client that will establish a connection with the local MQTT server and then will make the client subscribe to the topic filter specified after the `-t` option: `sensors/+/altitude`. We specify that we want to use QoS level 1 to subscribe to the topic filter with the `-q 1` option. We specify the `-d` option to enable debug messages that will allow us to understand what happens under the hood and the differences when compared with publishing a message with QoS level 0.

The Terminal or Command Prompt window will display debug messages similar to the following lines. Take into account that the generated `ClientId` will be different from the one shown after `Client mosqsub|16736-LAPTOP-5D`. Notice that `QoS: 1` indicates that the subscription is done with QoS level 1:

```
Client mosqsub|16736-LAPTOP-5D sending CONNECT
Client mosqsub|16736-LAPTOP-5D received CONNACK
Client mosqsub|16736-LAPTOP-5D sending SUBSCRIBE (Mid: 1, Topic:
sensors/+/altitude, QoS: 1)
Client mosqsub|16736-LAPTOP-5D received SUBACK
Subscribed (mid: 1): 1
```

We will use the `mosquitto_pub` command-line utility included in Mosquitto to generate a simple MQTT client that publishes a message to a topic with QoS level 1 instead of the QoS level 0 that we used when we published messages before. Open a Terminal in macOS or Linux, or a Command Prompt in Windows, go to the directory in which Mosquitto is installed, and run the following command:

```
mosquitto_pub -V mqttv311 -t sensors/hexacopter02/altitude -m  "75 f" -q 1
-d
```

The previous command will create an MQTT client that will establish a connection with the local MQTT server and then will make the client publish a message to the topic specified after the `-t` option: `sensors/hexacopter02/altitude`. We specify the payload for the message after the `-m` option: `"75 f"`. We specify that we want to use QoS level 1 to publish the message with the `-q 1` option. We specify the X option to enable debug messages that will allow us to understand what happens under the hood and the differences when compared with publishing a message with QoS level 0.

The Terminal or Command Prompt window will display debug messages similar to the following lines. Take into account that the generated `ClientId` will be different from the one shown after `Client mosqpub|19544-LAPTOP-5D`. After publishing the message, the client disconnects:

```
Client mosqpub|19544-LAPTOP-5D sending CONNECT
Client mosqpub|19544-LAPTOP-5D received CONNACK
Client mosqpub|19544-LAPTOP-5D sending PUBLISH (d0, q1, r0, m1,
'sensors/drone02/altitude', ... (4 bytes))
Client mosqpub|19544-LAPTOP-5D received PUBACK (Mid: 1)
Client mosqpub|19544-LAPTOP-5D sending DISCONNECT
```

The previous lines show that the generated MQTT client sends a PUBLISH packet to the MQTT server and then receives a PUBACK package from the server.

Now, go back to the Terminal or Command Prompt window in which you executed the mosquitto_sub command and subscribed to the sensors/+/atitude topic filter. You will see lines similar to the following ones:

```
Client mosqsub|16736-LAPTOP-5D received PUBLISH (d0, q1, r0, m1,
'sensors/drone02/altitude', ... (4 bytes))
Client mosqsub|16736-LAPTOP-5D sending PUBACK (Mid: 1)
75 f
```

The previous lines show that the generated MQTT client, that is, the subscriber, received a PUBLISH packet from the MQTT server and then sent a PUBACK package to the server to acknowledge the message. If we clean up the debug messages that start with the Client prefix, we will see just the last line that shows the payloads for the message that we received as a result of our subscription to the sensors/+/altitude topic filter: 75 f.

The MQTT client that has already established a connection, that is, the publisher, sends a PUBLISH packet to the MQTT server with the header we have already described, QoS set to 1, and including a PacketId numeric value that will be unique for this client. At this time, the publisher will consider the PUBLISH packet identified with the PacketId as an unacknowledged PUBLISH packet.

The MQTT server reads a valid PUBLISH packet and it responds to the publisher with a PUBACK packet with the same PacketId value that has been used for the PUBLISH packet. Once the publisher receives the PUBACK packet, it discards the message and the MQTT server is responsible for publishing it to the appropriate subscribers.

The following diagram shows the interaction between a publisher and an MQTT server to publish a message with a QoS level of 1:

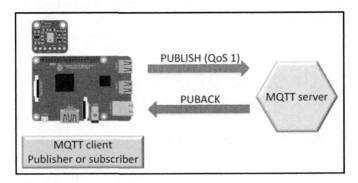

The MQTT server can start publishing messages to the appropriate subscribers before it sends the PUBACK packet to the publisher. Hence, when the publisher receives the PUBACK packet from the MQTT server, it doesn't mean that all the subscribers have received the message. It is very important to understand the meaning of this PUBACK packet.

For each subscriber to which the message has to be published, the MQTT server will send a PUBLISH packet and the subscriber must acknowledge receipt of the message by sending a PUBACK packet to the MQTT server. The following diagram shows the interaction between an MQTT server and the subscribers when a message is published with a QoS level of 1:

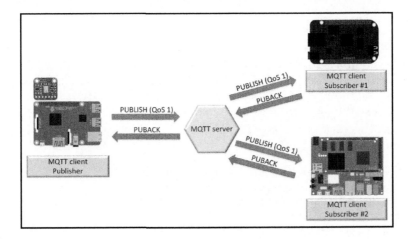

If the application is able to tolerate duplicates and we have to make sure that messages reach the subscribers at least once, QoS level 1 is an excellent choice. If there is no way to handle duplicates, we have to use QoS level 2.

Working with exactly once delivery (QoS level 2)

First, we will use wildcards to subscribe to a topic filter with QoS level 2, and then we will publish one message to a topic that will match the topic filter with QoS level 2. This way, we will analyze how both publishing and subscription work with QoS level 2.

We will use the `mosquitto_sub` command-line utility included in Mosquitto to generate a simple MQTT client that subscribes to a topic filter with QoS level 1 and prints all the messages it receives. Open a Terminal in macOS or Linux, or a Command Prompt in Windows, go to the directory in which Mosquitto is installed, and run the following command:

```
mosquitto_sub -V mqttv311 -t sensors/quadcopter30/# -q 2 -d
```

The previous command will create an MQTT client that will establish a connection with the local MQTT server and then will make the client subscribe to the topic filter specified after the `-t` option: `sensors/quadcopter30/#`. We specify that we want to use QoS level 2 to subscribe to the topic filter with the `-q 2` option. We specify the `-d` option to enable debug messages that will allow us to understand what happens under the hood and the differences when compared with publishing a message with QoS levels 0 and 1.

The Terminal or Command Prompt window will display debug messages similar to the following lines. Take into account that the generated `ClientId` will be different from the one shown after `Client mosqsub|8876-LAPTOP-5DO`. Notice that `QoS: 2` indicates that the subscription is done with QoS level 2:

```
Client mosqsub|8876-LAPTOP-5DO sending CONNECT
Client mosqsub|8876-LAPTOP-5DO received CONNACK
Client mosqsub|8876-LAPTOP-5DO sending SUBSCRIBE (Mid: 1, Topic:
sensors/quadcopter30/#, QoS: 2)
Client mosqsub|8876-LAPTOP-5DO received SUBACK
Subscribed (mid: 1): 2
```

We will use the `mosquitto_pub` command-line utility included in Mosquitto to generate a simple MQTT client that publishes a message to a topic with QoS level 2 instead of QoS levels 0 and 1 we used when we published messages before. Open a Terminal in macOS or Linux, or a Command Prompt in Windows, go to the directory in which Mosquitto is installed, and run the following command:

```
mosquitto_pub -V mqttv311 -t sensors/quadcopter30/speed/rotor/1 -m  "123 f"
-q 2 -d
```

The previous command will create an MQTT client that will establish a connection with the local MQTT server and then will make the client publish a message to the topic specified after the `-t` option: `sensors/quadcopter30/speed/rotor/1`. We specify the payload for the message after the `-m` option: `"123 f"`. We specify that we want to use QoS level 2 to publish the message with the `-q 2` option. We specify the `-d` option to enable debug messages that will allow us to understand what happens under the hood and the differences when compared with publishing a message with QoS levels 0 and 1.

The Terminal or Command Prompt window will display debug messages similar to the following lines. Take into account that the generated `ClientId` will be different from the one shown after `Client mosqpub|14652-LAPTOP-5D`. After publishing the message, the client disconnects:

```
Client mosqpub|14652-LAPTOP-5D sending CONNECT
Client mosqpub|14652-LAPTOP-5D received CONNACK
Client mosqpub|14652-LAPTOP-5D sending PUBLISH (d0, q2, r0, m1,
'sensors/quadcopter30/speed/rotor/1', ... (5 bytes))
Client mosqpub|14652-LAPTOP-5D received PUBREC (Mid: 1)
Client mosqpub|14652-LAPTOP-5D sending PUBREL (Mid: 1)
Client mosqpub|14652-LAPTOP-5D received PUBCOMP (Mid: 1)
Client mosqpub|14652-LAPTOP-5D sending DISCONNECT
```

The previous lines show that the generated MQTT client, that is, the publisher, had the following packet exchanges with the MQTT server:

1. The publisher sent a PUBLISH packet to the MQTT server
2. The publisher received a PUBREC packet from the MQTT server
3. The publisher sent a PUBREL packet to the MQTT server
4. The publisher received a PUBCOMP packet from the MQTT server

Now, go back to the Terminal or Command Prompt window in which you executed the `mosquitto_sub` command and subscribed to the `sensors/quadcopter30/#` topic filter. You will see lines similar to the following ones:

```
Client mosqsub|8876-LAPTOP-5DO received PUBLISH (d0, q2, r0, m1,
'sensors/quadcopter30/speed/rotor/1', ... (5 bytes))
Client mosqsub|8876-LAPTOP-5DO sending PUBREC (Mid: 1)
Client mosqsub|8876-LAPTOP-5DO received PUBREL (Mid: 1)
123 f
Client mosqsub|8876-LAPTOP-5DO sending PUBCOMP (Mid: 1)
```

The previous lines show that the generated MQTT client, that is, the subscriber, had the following packet exchanges with the MQTT server:

1. The subscriber received a PUBLISH packet from the MQTT server
2. The subscriber sent a PUBREC packet to the MQTT server
3. The subscriber received a PUBREL packet from the MQTT server
4. The subscriber sent a PUBCOMP packet to the MQTT server after it successfully received the message with the payload

If we clean up debug messages that start with the `Client` prefix, we will see just the last line, which shows the payloads for the message which we received as a result of our subscription to the `sensors/quadcopter30/#` topic filter: `123 f`.

The MQTT client that has already established a connection, that is, the publisher sends a PUBLISH packet to the MQTT server with the header we have already described, QoS set to 2, and including a `PacketId` numeric value that will be unique for this client. At this time, the publisher will consider the PUBLISH packet identified with the `PacketId` as an unacknowledged PUBLISH packet.

The MQTT server reads a valid PUBLISH packet and it will respond to the publisher with a PUBREC packet with the same `PacketId` value that has been used for the PUBLISH packet. The PUBREC packet indicates that the MQTT server accepted the ownership of the message. Once the publisher receives the PUBREC packet, it discards the message and it stores the `PacketId` related to the message and the PUBREC packet.

The publisher sends a PUBREL packet to the MQTT server as a response to the received PUBREC packet. This PUBREL packet will be considered unacknowledged until it receives the PUBCOMP packet related to the `PacketId` from the MQTT server. Finally, the MQTT server sends a PUBCOMP packet with the `PacketId` to the publisher and, at this point, both the publisher and the MQTT server are sure that the message has been successfully delivered.

The following diagram shows the interaction between a publisher and an MQTT server to publish a message with a QoS level of 2:

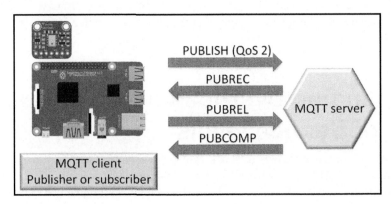

For each subscriber with QoS level 2 to which the message has to be published, the MQTT server will send a PUBLISH packet, and the same packet exchange that we have analyzed between the publisher and the MQTT server will happen between the MQTT server and the subscriber. However, in this case, the MQTT server is the one that acts as a publisher and starts the flow. The following diagram shows the interaction between an MQTT server and the subscribers when a message is published with a QoS level of 2:

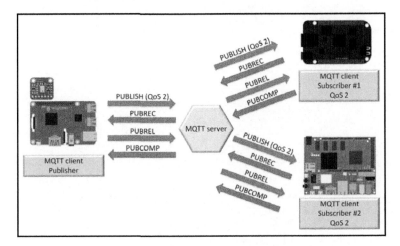

If the application isn't able to tolerate duplicates and we have to make sure that messages reach the subscribers only once, QoS level 2 is the appropriate choice. However, magic comes with a price: we must take into account that QoS level 2 has the highest overhead compared to the other QoS levels.

Understanding overhead in the different Quality of Service levels

The following diagram summarizes the different packages that are exchanged between an MQTT client and an MQTT server to publish a message with QoS levels 0, 1, and 2. This way, we can easily recognize the increased overhead as we increase the QoS level:

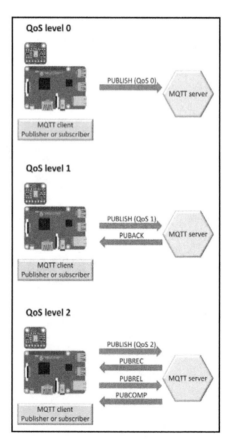

It is very important to take into account the additional overhead required by QoS level 2 and to use it only when it is really necessary.

Test your knowledge

Let's see whether you can answer the following questions correctly:

1. QoS level 0 for MQTT means:
    1. Exactly once delivery
    2. At most once delivery
    3. At least once delivery

2. QoS level 1 for MQTT means:
    1. Exactly once delivery
    2. At most once delivery
    3. At least once delivery

3. QoS level 2 for MQTT means:
    1. Exactly once delivery
    2. At most once delivery
    3. At least once delivery

4. If the application isn't able to tolerate duplicates and we have to make sure that the messages reach the subscribers only once, the appropriate choice is:
    1. QoS level 0
    2. QoS level 1
    3. QoS level 2

5. Which QoS level has the highest overhead:
    1. QoS level 0
    2. QoS level 1
    3. QoS level 2

The rights answers are included in the `Appendix`, *Solutions*.

Summary

In this chapter, we worked with different tools to interact with the Mosquitto MQTT 3.1.1 server we installed in Chapter 1, *Installing an MQTT 3.1.1 Mosquitto Server*. We worked with an unsecured MQTT server to easily understand the interaction between the MQTT clients and the MQTT server.

We subscribed to topics via the command-line and GUI tools. Then, we published messages with QoS level 0 and we unsubscribed from topics. We learned best practices related to topics; and single-level, and multilevel wildcards. We studied in detail the different Quality of Service levels supported by MQTT and when it is appropriate to use each of them. We analyzed their advantages and disadvantages.

Now that we understood how the MQTT 3.1.1 basics work, we will learn how to secure an MQTT server and to follow best practices related to security, which are the topics that we are going to discuss in Chapter 3, *Securing an MQTT 3.1.1 Mosquitto Server*.

3
Securing an MQTT 3.1.1 Mosquitto Server

In this chapter, we will secure an MQTT 3.1.1 Mosquitto server. We will make all the configurations required to work with digital certificates to encrypt all the data sent between MQTT clients and the server. We will use TLS and we will learn to work with client certificates for each MQTT client. We will also learn to force the desired TLS protocol version. We will gain an understanding of the following:

- The importance of securing a Mosquitto server
- Generating a private certificate authority to use TLS with Mosquitto
- Creating a certificate for the Mosquitto server
- Configuring TLS transport security in Mosquitto
- Testing the MQTT TLS configuration with command-line tools
- Testing the MQTT TLS configuration with GUI tools
- Creating a certificate for each MQTT client
- Configuring TLS client certificate authentication in Mosquitto
- Testing the MQTT TLS client authentication with command-line tools
- Testing the MQTT TLS configuration with GUI tools
- Forcing the TLS protocol version to a specific number

Understanding the importance of securing a Mosquitto server

Security for IoT applications is an extremely important topic that deserves many entire books dedicated to it. Each solution has its own security requirements and it is very important to consider all of them when developing each component of the solution.

If we use MQTT to publish values that are neither confidential nor critical for other applications, our only concern might be to keep control of the maximum number of subscribers to each topic to make sure messages are always available. This way, we can prevent the MQTT server failing to deliver messages to a huge number of subscribers.

However, most of the time we won't be working on a solution that can share data with the entire world without limitations and doesn't need to care about data confidentiality and integrity, in addition to data availability. Imagine that we are working on a solution that allows users to control a huge octocopter drone. If the drone flies the wrong way, we can do harm to real people. We cannot allow any unknown publisher to be able to send messages to the topics that allow us to control the octocopter. We have to make sure that the right person is controlling the octocopter and that commands sent as part of messages cannot be altered by an intruder in the middle; that is, we need data integrity.

The different levels of security come at a price; that is, there is always an additional overhead. Hence, we should always keep a balance to avoid overheads that can make the entire solution unfeasible and unusable. Whenever we add more security, we will require additional bandwidth and we will add a processing overhead in the clients and the server. We have to take into account that some cryptographic algorithms that work without problems in modern smartphones aren't suitable for IoT boards with constrained processing power. Sometimes, security requirements can force us to use specific hardware, such as more powerful IoT boards. We definitely have to consider security before purchasing all the hardware for our solution.

Another important thing that we must take into account is that many security levels require maintenance tasks that might be unfeasible in certain cases or extremely difficult to achieve in other cases. For example, if we decide to use a certificate for each device that will become a client of the MQTT server, we will have to generate and distribute a certificate for each device. We have to access the filesystem for the device to copy new files to it. If we have to invalidate a certificate, it will be necessary to provide a new certificate to the affected device. Consider a situation in which all devices are distributed in different locations that are difficult to access; we must have a mechanism to remotely access a device and be able to provide it with the new certificate. This task will also require security because we don't want anybody to access the device's filesystem. Thus, things can become extremely complex once we start analyzing all the security requirements and possible and necessary maintenance tasks.

Each MQTT server or broker implementation can provide specific security features. We will work with some of the features provided by Mosquitto out of the box. Specific security requirements might make us decide to work with a specific MQTT server or broker implementation.

When we work with Mosquitto, we can implement security at the following levels:

- **Network**: We can use a **VPN** (short for **virtual private network**) to extend a private network across the internet.
- **Transport**: MQTT uses TCP as the transport protocol, and therefore by default communications aren't encrypted. **TLS** (short for **Transport Layer Security**) is usually referred to as TLS/SSL because **SSL** (short for **Secure Socket Layers**) is its predecessor. We can use TLS to secure and encrypt communications between MQTT clients and the MQTT server. The use of TLS with MQTT is sometimes referred to as MQTTS. TLS allows us to provide both privacy and data integrity. We can use TLS client certificates to provide authentication.
- **Application**: At this level, we can take advantage of features included in MQTT to provide application-level authentication and authorization. We can use the `ClientId` (client identifier) to identify each client and combine it with user name and password authentication. We can add additional security mechanisms at this level. For example, we can encrypt the message payload and/or add integrity checks to ensure data integrity. However, the topic will still be unencrypted, and therefore TLS is the only way of making sure everything is encrypted. We can work with plugins to provide more complex authentication and authorization mechanisms. We can grant or deny permissions to each user to control which topics they can subscribe to and which topics they can publish messages to.

Most popular MQTT implementations provide support for TLS. However, make sure that you check the features before selecting the appropriate MQTT server for your solution.

We won't cover all security topics, because it would require one or more entire books dedicated to these topics. Instead, we will focus on the most common features used in transport-level security first and then we will move on to application-level security. The use of VPNs is beyond the scope globally of this book. However, you must consider their use based on your specific needs. We will use Mosquitto for our examples, but you can follow many similar procedures for any other MQTT server you decide to use. Everything we will learn will be useful for any other MQTT server that provides support for the same security features that we will use with Mosquitto.

Generating a private certificate authority to use TLS with Mosquitto

So far, we have been working with a Mosquitto server with its default configuration, which listens on port 1883 and uses plain TCP as the transport protocol. The data sent between each MQTT client and the MQTT server isn't encrypted. There are no restrictions on subscribers or publishers. If we open firewall ports and redirect ports in the router, or we configure port securities for a cloud-based virtual machine in which the MQTT server is running, any MQTT client that has the IP address or host name for the MQTT server can publish to any topic and can subscribe to any topic.

In our examples in Chapter 2, *Using Command-Line and GUI Tools to Learn How MQTT Works*, we haven't made any changes in our configurations to allow incoming connections to port 1883, and therefore we haven't opened our Mosquitto server to the internet.

We want to use TLS with MQTT and Mosquitto in our development environment. This way, we will make sure that we can trust the MQTT server because we have confidence it is who it says it is, our data will be private because it will be encrypted, and it will have integrity because it won't be altered. If you have experience with the *HTTP* protocol, you'll recognize that we make the same shift we do when we move from using *HTTP* to *HTTPS*.

Websites purchase certificates from major certificate authorities. If we want to use a purchased certificate for the server, we don't need to generate our own certificates. In fact, it is the most convenient option when we have an MQTT server made public and we move to a production environment.

In this case, we will use the free OpenSSL utility to generate the necessary certificates for the server to enable TLS with Mosquitto for our development environment. It is very important to notice that we won't generate a production-ready configuration and we are focusing on a secure development environment that will mimic a secure production environment.

OpenSSL is already installed in macOS and most modern Linux distributions. In Windows, we have already installed OpenSSL as one of the prerequisites for Mosquitto. The use of the OpenSSL utility deserves an entire book, and therefore we will just focus on generating the certificate we need with the most common options. If you have specific security needs, make sure you explore the necessary options to achieve your goals with OpenSSL.

Specifically, we will generate an X.509 digital certificate that uses the X.509 **PKI** (short for **public key infrastructure**) standard. This digital certificate allows us to confirm that a specific public key belongs to the subject included within the certificate. There is an identity that issues the certificate and its details are also included in the certificate.

The digital certificate is valid only within a specific period, and therefore we must take into account that a digital certificate will expire some day and we will have to provide a new certificate to replace the expired one. There are specific data requirements for certificates based on the specific X.509 version that we use. According to the version and to the options we use to generate the certificates, we might need to provide specific data.

We will be running commands to generate different X.509 digital certificates and we will provide all the necessary details that will be included in the certificate. We will understand all the data that the certificate will have when we create it.

We will create our own private certificate authority, also known as a CA. We will create a root certificate and then we will generate the server key.

Check the directory or folder in which you installed OpenSSL.

On macOS, OpenSSL is installed in `/usr/bin/openssl`. However, it is an old version and it is necessary to install a newer version before running the commands. It is possible to install the new version with the `homebrew` package manager and you will be able to run the new version in another directory. For example, the path for version 1.0.2n, installed with `homebrew`, will be in `/usr/local/Cellar/openssl/1.0.2n/bin/openssl`. Make sure you don't use the default old version.

In Windows, the OpenSSL version we installed as a prerequisite for Mosquitto, in Chapter 2, *Using Command-Line and GUI Tools to Learn How MQTT Works*, has the `openssl.exe` executable file in the default `C:\OpenSSL-Win32\bin` folder. If you are working with Windows, you can use either the Command Prompt or Windows PowerShell.

In any operating system, use the full path to the appropriate OpenSSL version in each of the next commands that start with `openssl`.

Create a new directory named `mosquitto_certificates` and change the necessary permissions for this directory to make sure that you can only access its contents.

Open a Terminal in macOS or Linux, or a Command Prompt in Windows, and go to the previously created directory, `mosquitto_certificates`. Run the following command to create a 2,048-bit root key and save it in the `ca.key` file:

```
openssl genrsa -out ca.key 2048
```

The following lines show sample output generated by the previous command:

```
Generating RSA private key, 2048 bit long modulus
......+++
.............+++
e is 65537 (0x010001)
```

The previous command will generate the private root key in the `ca.key` file. Make sure you keep this file private because anybody that has this file will be able to generate certificates. It is also possible to password-protect this file by using other options with `openssl`. However, as previously explained, we will follow the necessary steps to use TLS and you can explore additional options related to OpenSSL and certificates.

Go to the Terminal in macOS or Linux, or the Command Prompt in Windows. Run the following command to self-sign the root certificate. The next command uses the previously created 2,048-bit private key saved in the `ca.key` file and generates a `ca.crt` file with the self-signed X.509 digital certificate. The command makes the self-signed certificate valid for `3650` days. The value is specified after the `-days` option:

```
openssl req -x509 -new -nodes -key ca.key -sha256 -days 3650 -out ca.crt
```

In this case, we specified the `-sha256` option to use SHA-256 hash functions. If we want increased security, we can use the `-sha512` instead option of `-sha256` in all cases in which we are using `-sha256`. This way, we will use SHA-512 hash functions. However, we must take into account that SHA-512 might not be appropriate for certain power-constrained IoT devices.

After you enter the previous command, OpenSSL asks for information that will be incorporated into the certificate. You have to enter the information and press *Enter*. If you don't want to enter specific information, just enter a dot (.) and press *Enter*. It is possible to pass all the values as arguments for the `openssl` command, but it makes it a bit difficult to understand what we are doing. In fact, it is also possible to use fewer calls to the `openssl` command to perform the previous tasks. However, we run a few more steps to understand what we are doing.

The following lines show sample output and questions with sample answers. Remember that we are generating our private certificate authority:

```
You are about to be asked to enter information that will be incorporated
into your certificate request.
What you are about to enter is what is called a Distinguished Name or a DN.
There are quite a few fields but you can leave some blank
For some fields there will be a default value,
If you enter '.', the field will be left blank.
-----
Country Name (2 letter code) [AU]:US
State or Province Name (full name) [Some-State]:NEW YORK CITY
Locality Name (eg, city) []:NEW YORK
Organization Name (eg, company) [Internet Widgits Pty Ltd]:MOSQUITTO
CERTIFICATE AUTHORITY
Organizational Unit Name (eg, section) []:
Common Name (e.g. server FQDN or YOUR name) []:MOSQUITTO CERTIFICATE
AUTHORITY
Email Address []:mosquittoca@example.com
```

Run the following command to display the data and details for the recently generated certificate authority certificate file:

```
Certificate:
    Data:
        Version: 3 (0x2)
        Serial Number:
            96:f6:f6:36:ad:63:b2:1f
        Signature Algorithm: sha256WithRSAEncryption
        Issuer: C = US, ST = NEW YORK, L = NEW YORK, O = MOSQUITTO
        CERTIFICATE AUTHORITY, CN = MOSQUITTO CERTIFICATE AUTHORITY,
        emailAddress = mosquittoca@example.com
        Validity
            Not Before: Mar 22 15:43:23 2018 GMT
            Not After : Mar 19 15:43:23 2028 GMT
            Subject: C = US, ST = NEW YORK, L = NEW YORK, O = MOSQUITTO
            CERTIFICATE AUTHORITY, CN = MOSQUITTO CERTIFICATE
            AUTHORITY, emailAddress = mosquittoca@example.com
```

```
Subject Public Key Info:
Public Key Algorithm: rsaEncryption
    Public-Key: (2048 bit)
    Modulus:
        00:c0:45:aa:43:d4:76:e7:dc:58:9b:19:85:5d:35:
        54:2f:58:61:72:6a:42:81:f9:64:1b:51:18:e1:95:
        ba:50:99:56:c5:9a:c2:fe:07:8e:26:12:47:a6:be:
        8b:ce:23:bf:4e:5a:ea:ab:2e:51:99:0f:23:ea:38:
        68:f3:80:16:5d:5f:51:cf:ce:ee:c9:e9:3a:34:ac:
        ee:24:a6:50:31:59:c5:db:75:b3:33:0e:96:31:23:
        1b:9c:6f:2f:96:1f:6d:cc:5c:4e:20:10:9e:f2:4e:
        a9:f6:31:83:54:11:b6:af:86:0e:e0:af:69:a5:b3:
        f2:5a:b5:da:b6:64:73:87:86:bb:e0:be:b3:10:9f:
        ef:91:8f:e5:68:8c:ab:38:75:8d:e1:33:bc:fb:00:
        d8:d6:d2:d3:6e:e3:a0:3f:08:b6:9e:d6:da:94:ad:
        61:74:90:6c:71:98:88:e8:e1:2b:2d:b1:18:bb:6d:
        b8:65:43:cf:ac:79:ab:a7:a4:3b:65:a8:8a:6f:be:
        c1:66:71:d6:9c:2d:d5:0e:81:13:69:23:65:fa:d3:
        cb:79:e5:75:ea:a2:22:72:c7:e4:f7:5c:be:e7:64:
        9b:54:17:dd:ca:43:7f:93:be:b6:39:20:e7:f1:21:
        0f:a7:e6:24:99:57:9b:02:1b:6d:e4:e5:ee:ad:76:
        2f:69
    Exponent: 65537 (0x10001)
    X509v3 extensions:
    X509v3 Subject Key Identifier:
F7:C7:9E:9D:D9:F2:9D:38:2F:7C:A6:8F:C5:07:56:57:48:7D:07:35
    X509v3 Authority Key Identifier:
keyid:F7:C7:9E:9D:D9:F2:9D:38:2F:7C:A6:8F:C5:07:56:57:48:7D:07:35
    X509v3 Basic Constraints: critical
        CA:TRUE
Signature Algorithm: sha256WithRSAEncryption
    a2:64:5d:7b:f4:85:81:f7:d0:30:8b:8d:7c:83:83:63:2c:4e:
    a8:56:fb:fc:f0:4f:d4:d8:9c:cd:ac:c7:e9:bc:4b:b5:87:9e:
    02:0b:9f:e0:4b:a3:da:3f:84:b4:1c:e3:42:d4:9f:4e:c0:29:
    f7:ae:18:d3:2d:bf:93:e2:2b:5c:d9:9a:82:53:d8:6a:fb:c8:
    47:9f:02:d4:05:11:e9:8f:2a:54:09:c4:a4:f1:00:eb:35:1d:
    6b:e9:55:3b:4b:a6:27:d0:52:cf:86:c1:03:32:ce:22:41:55:
    32:1e:93:4f:6b:a5:b5:19:9e:8c:a7:de:91:2b:2c:c6:95:a9:
    b6:44:18:e7:40:23:38:87:5d:89:b6:25:d7:32:60:28:0b:41:
    5b:6e:46:20:bf:36:9d:ba:26:6d:63:71:0f:fd:c3:e3:0d:6b:
    b6:84:34:06:ea:67:7c:4e:2e:df:fe:b6:ec:48:f5:7b:b5:06:
    c5:ad:6f:3e:0c:25:2b:a3:9d:49:f7:d4:b7:69:9e:3e:ca:f8:
    65:f2:77:ae:50:63:2b:48:e0:72:93:a7:60:99:b7:40:52:ab:
    6f:00:78:89:ad:92:82:93:e3:30:ab:ac:24:e7:82:7f:51:c7:
    2d:e7:e1:2d:3f:4d:c1:5c:27:15:d9:bc:81:7b:00:a0:75:07:
    99:ee:78:70
```

After running the previous commands, we will have the following two files in the `mqtt_certificates` directory:

- `ca.key`: Certificate authority key
- `ca.crt`: Certificate authority certificate file

> The certificate authority certificate file is in the **PEM** (short for **privacy enhanced mail**) format. We must remember this format because some MQTT utilities will require us to specify whether the certificate is in PEM format or not. A wrong value in this option won't allow the MQTT client to establish a connection with an MQTT server that uses a certificate in PEM format.

Creating a certificate for the Mosquitto server

Now that we have a private certificate authority, we can create the certificate for the Mosquitto server, that is, a certificate for the computer that will run the MQTT server.

First, we must generate a new private key that will be different from the private key we generated for our own private certificate authority.

Go to the Terminal in macOS or Linux, or the Command Prompt in Windows. Run the following command to create a 2,048-bit key and save it in the `server.key` file:

```
openssl genrsa -out server.key 2048
```

The following lines show sample output generated by the previous command:

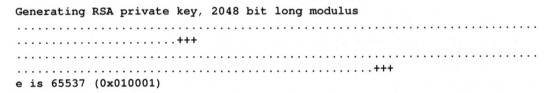

```
Generating RSA private key, 2048 bit long modulus
..............................................................
.....................+++
..............................................................
...................................................+++
e is 65537 (0x010001)
```

The previous command will generate the private key in the `server.key` file. Go back to the Terminal in macOS or Linux, or the Command Prompt in Windows. Run the following command to generate a certificate signing request. The next command uses the previously created 2,048-bit private key saved in the `server.key` file and generates a `server.csr` file:

```
openssl req -new -key server.key -out server.csr
```

After you enter the previous command, OpenSSL asks for information that will be incorporated in the certificate. You have to enter the information and press *Enter*. If you don't want to enter specific information, just enter a dot (`.`) and press *Enter*. In this case, the most important value is **Common Name**. Enter the IPv4 or IPv6 address for the computer that is running the Mosquitto server in this field instead of the `192.168.1.1` value shown in the next lines. The following lines show the sample output and questions with sample answers. Do not forget to enter the appropriate value for **Common Name**:

```
You are about to be asked to enter information that will be incorporated
into your certificate request.
What you are about to enter is what is called a Distinguished Name or a DN.
There are quite a few fields but you can leave some blank
For some fields there will be a default value,
If you enter '.', the field will be left blank.
-----
Country Name (2 letter code) [AU]:US
State or Province Name (full name) [Some-State]:FLORIDA
Locality Name (eg, city) []:ORLANDO
Organization Name (eg, company) [Internet Widgits Pty Ltd]:MQTT 3.1.1
SERVER
Organizational Unit Name (eg, section) []:MQTT
Common Name (e.g. server FQDN or YOUR name) []:192.168.1.1
Email Address []:mosquittoserver@example.com

Please enter the following 'extra' attributes
to be sent with your certificate request
A challenge password []:
An optional company name []:Mosquitto MQTT Server
```

Go to the Terminal in macOS or Linux, or the Command Prompt in Windows. Run the following command to sign the previously created certificate signing request, that is, the `server.csr` file. The next command also uses the self-signed X.509 digital certificate for the certificate authority and its private key that we generated before: the `ca.crt` and `ca.key` files.

The command generates a `server.crt` file with the signed X.509 digital certificate for the Mosquitto server. The command makes the signed certificate valid for 3,650 days. The value is specified after the `-days` option:

```
openssl x509 -req -in server.csr -CA ca.crt -CAkey ca.key -CAcreateserial -
out server.crt -days 3650 -sha256
```

As happened when we created the self-signed X.509 digital certificate for the certificate authority, we also specify the `-sha256` option to use SHA-256 hash functions for the Mosquitto server certificate. You can use `-sha512` instead option of `-sha256` if you want to use SHA-512 hash functions for increased security.

The following lines show sample output generated by the previous command. The values shown after `subject` will be different in your configuration because you entered your own values when you generated the certificate signing request that was saved in the `server.csr` file:

```
Signature ok
subject=C = US, ST = FLORIDA, L = ORLANDO, O = MQTT 3.1.1 SERVER, OU =
MQTT, CN = 192.168.1.1, emailAddress = mosquittoserver@example.com
Getting CA Private Key
```

Run the following command to display data and details for the generated server certificate file:

```
openssl x509 -in server.crt -noout -text
```

The following lines show sample output that displays details about the signature algorithm, the issuer, the validity, the subject, and the signature algorithms:

```
Certificate:
    Data:
        Version: 1 (0x0)
        Serial Number:
            a1:fa:a7:26:53:da:24:0b
    Signature Algorithm: sha256WithRSAEncryption
        Issuer: C = US, ST = NEW YORK, L = NEW YORK, O = MOSQUITTO
        CERTIFICATE AUTHORITY, CN = MOSQUITTO CERTIFICATE AUTHORITY,
        emailAddress = mosquittoca@example.com
        Validity
            Not Before: Mar 22 18:20:01 2018 GMT
            Not After : Mar 19 18:20:01 2028 GMT
        Subject: C = US, ST = FLORIDA, L = ORLANDO, O = MQTT 3.1.1
        SERVER, OU = MQTT, CN = 192.168.1.1, emailAddress =
        mosquittoserver@example.com
```

```
Subject Public Key Info:
    Public Key Algorithm: rsaEncryption
        Public-Key: (2048 bit)
        Modulus:
            00:f5:8b:3e:76:0a:ab:65:d2:ee:3e:47:6e:dc:be:
            74:7e:96:5c:93:25:45:54:a4:97:bc:4d:34:3b:ed:
            33:89:39:f4:df:8b:cd:9f:63:fa:4d:d4:01:c8:a5:
            0b:4f:c7:0d:35:a0:9a:20:4f:66:be:0e:4e:f7:1a:
            bc:4a:86:a7:1f:69:30:36:01:2f:93:e6:ff:8f:ca:
            1f:d0:58:fa:37:e0:90:5f:f8:06:7c:2c:1c:c7:21:
            c8:b4:12:d4:b7:b1:4e:5e:6d:41:68:f3:dd:03:33:
            f5:d5:e3:de:37:08:c4:5f:8c:db:21:a2:d7:20:12:
            f2:a4:81:20:3d:e4:d7:af:81:32:82:31:a2:2b:fd:
            02:c2:ee:a0:fa:53:1b:ca:2d:43:b3:7e:b7:b8:12:
            9c:3e:26:66:cd:90:34:ba:aa:6b:ad:e4:eb:0d:15:
            cf:0b:ce:f6:b1:07:1f:7c:33:05:11:4b:57:6c:48:
            0d:f8:e5:f3:d3:f0:88:92:53:ec:3e:04:d7:fc:81:
            75:5e:ef:01:56:f1:66:fe:a4:34:9b:13:8a:b6:5d:
            cc:8f:72:11:0e:9c:c9:65:71:e3:dd:0e:5a:b7:9d:
            8f:18:3e:09:62:52:5f:fa:a5:96:4d:2b:35:23:26:
            ca:74:5d:f9:04:64:f1:f8:f6:f6:7a:d7:31:4c:b7:
            e8:53
        Exponent: 65537 (0x10001)
    Signature Algorithm: sha256WithRSAEncryption
    9c:2f:b5:f9:fa:06:9f:a3:1e:a3:38:94:a7:aa:4c:11:e9:30:
    2e:4b:cf:16:a3:c6:46:ad:e5:3b:d9:43:f0:41:37:62:93:94:
    72:56:1a:dd:27:50:f7:89:2f:4b:56:55:59:d6:da:2e:8f:0a:
    d8:1e:dd:41:0e:1c:36:1b:eb:8d:32:2c:24:ef:58:93:18:e1:
    fc:ce:71:f6:b2:ed:84:5e:06:52:b8:f1:87:f3:13:ca:b9:41:
    3f:a2:1d:a0:52:5d:52:37:6c:2b:8c:28:ab:7f:7d:ed:fc:07:
    9f:60:8b:ad:3d:48:17:95:fe:20:b8:96:87:44:9a:32:b8:9c:
    a8:d7:3c:cf:98:ba:a4:5c:c9:6e:0c:10:ee:45:3a:23:4a:e8:
    34:28:63:c4:8e:6e:1b:d9:a0:1b:e5:cc:33:69:ae:6f:e1:bb:
    99:df:04:fa:c9:bd:8c:c5:c7:e9:a9:fd:f2:dc:2c:b3:a9:7c:
    8a:ef:bf:66:f6:09:01:9a:0e:8f:27:a4:a1:45:f7:90:d2:bb:
    6d:4f:12:46:56:29:85:cd:c8:d6:d7:d3:60:e4:d1:27:a3:88:
    52:41:6a:7d:b2:06:8e:10:ec:ae:b5:7e:58:3e:ae:33:7c:f7:
    3a:21:a6:ae:61:5f:4d:c8:44:86:48:3d:c4:32:f2:db:05:e9:
    c9:f1:0c:be
```

After running the previous commands, we will have the following three files in the `mqtt_certificates` directory:

- `server.key`: Server key
- `server.csr`: Server certificate signing request
- `server.crt`: Server certificate file

The server certificate file is in PEM format, as is the certificate authority certificate file.

Configuring TLS transport security in Mosquitto

Now, we will configure Mosquitto to use TLS transport security and work with encrypted communications with different clients. Notice that we haven't generated certificates for the clients, and therefore we won't use client certificates for authentication. This way, any client that has the `ca.crt` file will be able to establish communication with the Mosquitto server.

Go to the Mosquitto installation directory and create a new sub-directory named `certificates`. In Windows, you will need administrator privileges to access the default installation folder.

Copy the following files from the `mqtt_certificates` directory, in which we saved the certificate authority certificate and the server certificate, to the `certificates` sub-directory we recently created within the Mosquitto installation directory:

- `ca.crt`
- `server.crt`
- `server.key`

If you are running the Mosquitto server in a Terminal window in macOS or Linux, press *Ctrl* + *C* to stop it. In Windows, stop the appropriate service by using the *Services* app. If you are running the Mosquitto server in Linux, run the following command to stop the service:

```
sudo service mosquitto stop
```

Go to the Mosquitto installation directory and open the `mosquitto.conf` configuration file with your favorite text editor. By default, all the lines for this file are commented out; that is, they start with a hash sign (#). The default value for each setting is indicated and includes the appropriate comments. This way, we easily know all the default values. The settings are organized in different sections.

It is good practice to make a backup copy of the exiting `mosquitto.conf` configuration file before making changes to it. Whenever we make changes to `mosquitto.conf`, it is a good idea to be able to easily roll back to the previous configuration if something goes wrong.

On macOS or Linux, add the following lines at the end of the configuration file and make sure you replace `/usr/local/etc/mosquitto/certificates` with the full path to the `certificates` directory we created within the `Mosquitto` installation folder:

```
# MQTT over TLS
listener 8883
cafile /usr/local/etc/mosquitto/certificates/ca.crt
certfile /usr/local/etc/mosquitto/certificates/server.crt
keyfile /usr/local/etc/mosquitto/certificates/server.key
```

In Windows, add the following lines at the end of the configuration file and make sure you replace `C:\Program Files (x86)\mosquitto\certificates` with the full path to the `certificates` directory we created within the `Mosquitto` installation folder. Notice that you will need administrator privileges when you run the text editor to open the file; that is, you will have to run the text editor as an administrator:

```
# MQTT over TLS
listener 8883
cafile C:\Program Files (x86)\mosquitto\certificates\ca.crt
certfile C:\Program Files (x86)\mosquitto\certificates\server.crt
keyfile C:\Program Files (x86)\mosquitto\certificates\server.key
```

We specified the `8883` value for the listener option to make Mosquitto listen for incoming network connections on TCP port number `8883`. This port is the default port number for MQTT with TLS.

The `cafile` option specifies the full path for the file that provides a PEM-encoded certificate authority certificate file: `ca.crt`.

The `certfile` option specifies the full path for the file that provides a PEM encoded server certificate: `server.crt`.

Finally, the `keyfile` option specifies the full path for the file that provides a PEM-encoded server keyfile: `server.key`.

Save the changes to the `mosquitto.conf` configuration file and launch Mosquitto again with the same mechanism we learned for Linux, macOS, and Windows in the previous chapter. The Mosquitto server will be listening on port `8883` instead of `1883`.

Testing the MQTT TLS configuration with command-line tools

We will use the `mosquitto_sub` command-line utility included in Mosquitto to try to generate a simple MQTT client that subscribes to a topic and prints all the messages it receives. We will use the default configuration, to try to establish a communication with the Mosquitto server, by using the default `1883` port without a certificate authority certificate specified. Open a Terminal in macOS or Linux, or a Command Prompt in Windows, go to the directory in which Mosquitto is installed, and run the following command:

```
mosquitto_sub -V mqttv311 -t sensors/octocopter01/altitude -d
```

The `mosquitto_sub` utility will display the following error. The Mosquitto server is not accepting any connections on port `1883` anymore. Notice that the error message might be different depending on the platform:

```
Error: No connection could be made because the target machine actively
refused it.
```

Run the following command using the `-p` option, followed by the port number that we want to use: `8883`. This way, we will try to connect to port `8883` instead of the default port `1883`:

```
mosquitto_sub -V mqttv311 -p 8883 -t sensors/octocopter01/altitude -d
```

The `mosquitto_sub` utility will display debug messages indicating it is sending the CONNECT packet to the MQTT server. However, the connection will never be established because the potential MQTT client isn't providing the required certificate authority. Press *Ctrl + C* to stop the utility trying to connect. The following lines show the sample output generated by the previous command:

```
Client mosqsub|14064-LAPTOP-5D sending CONNECT
Client mosqsub|14064-LAPTOP-5D sending CONNECT
Client mosqsub|14064-LAPTOP-5D sending CONNECT
Client mosqsub|14064-LAPTOP-5D sending CONNECT
Client mosqsub|14064-LAPTOP-5D sending CONNECT
Client mosqsub|14064-LAPTOP-5D sending CONNECT
```

The following command uses the -h option followed by the MQTT server host. In this case, we specify the IPv4 address of the computer that is running the Mosquitto MQTT server: 192.168.1.1. Notice that this value must match the IPv4 or IPv6 address that we specified as the value in the **Common Name** field when we generated the server.csr file, that is, the server certificate signing request. If you used a host name as the value in the **Common Name** field instead of an IPv4 or IPv6 address, you will have to use the same host name. If there is not match between the value specified for the -h option and the value indicated in the **Common Name** field, the Mosquitto server will reject the client. Thus, make sure you replace 192.168.1.1 in the next line with the appropriate value. In addition, the command specifies the certificate authority certificate file after the --cafile option and indicates that we want to use port 8883. You just have to replace ca.crt with the full path to the ca.crt file you created in the mqtt_certificates directory. For example, it might be C:\mqtt_certificates\ca.crt in Windows or /Users/gaston/mqtt_certificates/ca.crt in macOS or Linux. The mosquitto_sub utility will create an MQTT subscriber that will establish an encrypted connection with Mosquitto:

```
mosquitto_sub -h 192.168.1.1 -V mqttv311 -p 8883 --cafile ca.crt -t
sensors/octocopter01/altitude -d
```

If you specify a value for the -h option that doesn't match the value specified in the **Common Name** field when you generated the server.csr file, you will see the following error message as a result of the previous command:

```
Client mosqsub|14064-LAPTOP-5D sending CONNECT
Error: A TLS error occurred.
```

 If the command generates the previous error message, make sure you review the previous steps to generate the server.csr file. Make sure you don't use localhost as the value for the -h option.

With a similar syntax, we will use the mosquitto_pub command-line utility included in Mosquitto to generate a simple MQTT client that publishes a message to a topic, with an encrypted connection. Open a Terminal in macOS or Linux, or a Command Prompt in Windows, go to the directory in which Mosquitto is installed, and run the following command.

Remember to replace `192.168.1.1` in the next line with the appropriate value. In addition, replace `ca.crt` with the full path to the `ca.crt` file you created in the `mqtt_certificates` directory:

```
mosquitto_pub -h 192.168.1.1 -V mqttv311 -p 8883 --cafile ca.crt -t
sensors/octocopter01/altitude -m "123 f" -d
```

After the command publishes the message, you will see it in the window that used the `mosquitto_sub` command to subscribe to the `sensors/octocopter01/altitude` topic.

Testing the MQTT TLS configuration with GUI tools

Now, we will use the MQTT.fx GUI utility to generate another MQTT client that uses an encrypted connection to publish messages to the same topic: `sensors/octocopter01/altitude`. We have to make changes to the connection options to enable TLS and specify the certificate authority certificate file. Follow these steps:

1. Launch MQTT.fx, select **local mosquitto** in the drop-down located at the upper-left corner, and click on the configuration icon at the right-hand side of this drop-down and at the left-hand side of the **Connect** button. MQTT.fx will display the **Edit Connection Profiles** dialog box with different options for the connection profile named **local mosquitto**.

2. Go to the **Broker Address** textbox and enter the IPv4 or IPv6 address that we specified as the value in the **Common Name** field when we generated the `server.csr` file, that is, the server certificate signing request. If you used a host name as the value in the **Common Name** field instead of an IPv4 or IPv6 address, you will have to use the same host name. If there is no match between the value specified in **Broker Address** and the value indicated in the **Common Name** field, the Mosquitto server will reject the client.

3. Go to the **Broker Port** textbook and enter **8883**.

4. Click the **SSL/TLS** button.

5. Activate the **Enable SSL/TLS** checkbox.

6. Activate the **CA certificate file** radio button.

7. Enter or select the full path to the `ca.crt` file that you created in the `mqtt_certificates` folder in the **CA Certificate File** textbox and click **OK**. The following screenshot shows a dialog box with the selected options:

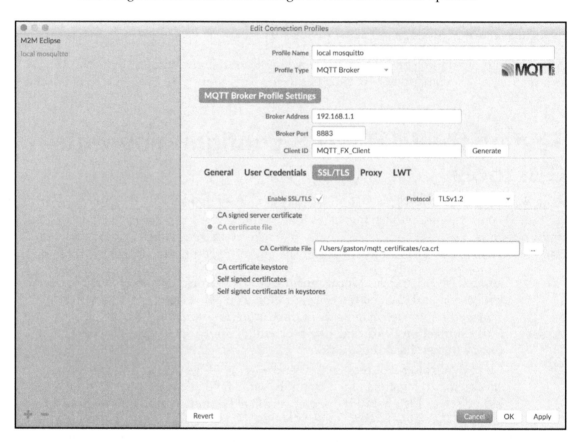

8. Click on the **Connect** button. MQTT.fx will establish an encrypted connection with the local Mosquitto server. Notice that the **Connect** button is disabled and the **Disconnect** button is enabled because the client is connected to the Mosquitto server.

9. Click **Subscribe** and enter `sensors/octocopter01/altitude` in the drop-down at the left-hand side of the **Subscribe** button. Then, click the **Subscribe** button. MQTT.fx will display a new panel at the left-hand side with the topic to which we have subscribed.

10. Click **Publish** and enter `sensors/octocopter01/altitude` in the drop-down at the left-hand side of the **Publish** button.

11. Enter the following text in the textbox below the **Publish** button: `250 f`.

12. Then, click the **Publish** button. MQTT.fx will publish the entered text to the specified topic.

13. Click **Subscribe** and you will see the published message.

With the configuration changes we have made to the Mosquitto server, any client that has the certificate authority certificate file, that is, the `ca.crt` file we generated, will be able to establish a connection with Mosquitto, subscribe, and publish to topics. The data sent between MQTT clients and the MQTT server is encrypted. In this configuration, we don't require the MQTT clients to provide certificates for authentication. However, don't forget that we are making configurations for our development environment. We should never use self-signed certificates for a production Mosquitto server.

There is another very popular GUI utility we can use to generate MQTT clients that can subscribe to topics and publish to topics: MQTT-spy. This utility is open source and can run on any computer that has Java 8 or higher installed on it. You can find more information about MQTT-spy here: `https://github.com/eclipse/paho.mqtt-spy`. The options to establish a connection with an MQTT server with a certificate authority certificate file are similar to the ones we analyzed for MQTT.fx. However, if you also want to work with this utility, it is convenient to analyze them in detail.

Now, we will use the MQTT-spy GUI utility to generate another MQTT client that uses an encrypted connection to publish messages to the same topic, `sensors/octocopter01/altitude`. Follow these steps:

1. Launch MQTT-spy.
2. Select **Connections** | **New connection**. The **Connection list** dialog box will appear.
3. Click on the **Connectivity** tab and select **MQTT 3.1.1** in the **Protocol version** drop-down. We want to work with MQTT version 3.1.1.
4. Go to the **Server URI(s)** textbox and enter the IPv4 or IPv6 address that we specified as the value in the **Common Name** field when we generated the `server.csr` file, that is, the server certificate signing request. If you used a host name as the value in the **Common Name** field instead of an IPv4 or IPv6 address, you will have to use the same host name. If there is not match between the value specified in **Broker Address** and the value indicated in the **Common Name** field, the Mosquitto server will reject the client generated by the MQTT-spy utility.
5. Click on the **Security** tab and in the **TLS** tab below the **User auth.** tab.
6. Select **CA certificate** in the **TLS/SSL mode** drop-down.
7. Select **TLSv1.2** in the **Protocol** drop-down.
8. Enter or select the full path to the `ca.crt` file that you created in the `mqtt_certificates` folder and click **Open** connection. The following screenshot shows the dialog box with the selected options:

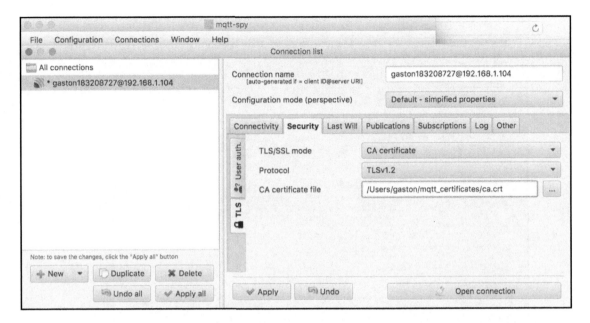

9. MQTT-spy will close the dialog box and will display a new tab with a green background and the connection name that has appeared highlighted and selected at the left-hand side in the **Connection list** dialog. Make sure you click on the tab for the new connection.

10. Enter `sensors/octocopter01/altitude` in the **Topic** drop-down.

11. Enter the following text in the **Data** textbox: 178 f. The following screenshot shows the tab for the new connection and the data entered in the different controls:

12. Click the **Publish** button. MQTT-spy will publish the entered text to the specified topic and you will be able to see the message in both the MQTT.fx subscriber and the mosquitto-sub subscriber.

Creating a certificate for each MQTT client

Now, we want to require each MQTT client to provide a valid certificate to establish a connection with the MQTT server. This way, only clients that have a valid certificate will be able to publish or subscribe to topics. We will use the previously created private certificate authority to create client certificates for authentication.

We will generate a sample certificate for our local computer that will act as a client. We can follow the same procedure to generate additional certificates for additional devices that we want to connect to the Mosquitto server. We just need to use a different name for the file and use a different device name in the corresponding option.

 We must use the same certificate authority certificate that we used to generate the server certificate to generate the client certificates. As previously explained, for a production environment we shouldn't use self-signed certificates. This procedure is useful for development environments.

First, we must generate a new private key that will be different from the private keys we generated for our own private certificate authority and for the server certificate.

Go to the Terminal in macOS or Linux, or the Command Prompt in Windows. Run the following command to create a 2,048-bit key and save it in the `board001.key` file. To repeat this procedure for other devices, replace `board001` with any other name that identifies the device that will use the certificate. Do this in all the following commands that use `board001` for different filenames and values:

```
openssl genrsa -out board001.key 2048
```

The following lines show sample output generated by the previous command:

```
Generating RSA private key, 2048 bit long modulus
.............................................................................
...............+++
.....................................+++
e is 65537 (0x10001)
```

The previous command will generate the private key in the `board001.key` file.

Go back to the Terminal in macOS or Linux, or the Command Prompt in Windows. Run the following command to generate a certificate-signing request, also known as CSR. The next command uses the previously created 2,048-bit private key saved in the `board001.key` file and generates a `board001.csr` file:

```
openssl req -new -key board001.key -out board001.csr
```

After you enter the previous command, OpenSSL asks for information that will be incorporated in the certificate. You have to enter the information and press *Enter*. If you don't want to enter specific information, just enter a dot (.) and press *Enter*. In this case, the most important value is **Common Name**. Enter the device name in this field:

```
You are about to be asked to enter information that will be incorporated
into your certificate request.
What you are about to enter is what is called a Distinguished Name or a DN.
There are quite a few fields but you can leave some blank
For some fields there will be a default value,
If you enter '.', the field will be left blank.
-----
Country Name (2 letter code) [AU]:US
State or Province Name (full name) [Some-State]:CALIFORNIA
Locality Name (eg, city) []:SANTA MONICA
Organization Name (eg, company) [Internet Widgits Pty Ltd]:MQTT BOARD 001
Organizational Unit Name (eg, section) []:MQTT BOARD 001
Common Name (e.g. server FQDN or YOUR name) []:MQTT BOARD 001
Email Address []:mttboard001@example.com

Please enter the following 'extra' attributes
to be sent with your certificate request
A challenge password []:.
An optional company name []:.
```

Go to the Terminal in macOS or Linux, or the Command Prompt in Windows. Run the following command to sign the previously created certificate signing request, that is, the `board001.csr` file. The next command also uses the self-signed X.509 digital certificate for the certificate authority and its private key that we generated before: the `ca.crt` and `ca.key` files. The command generates a `board001.crt` file with the signed X.509 digital certificate for the MQTT client. The command makes the signed certificate valid for 3,650 days, which is the value specified after the `-days` option. The `-addTrust clientAuth` option indicates that we want to use the certificate to authenticate a client:

```
openssl x509 -req -in board001.csr -CA ca.crt -CAkey ca.key -CAcreateserial
-out board001.crt -days 3650 -sha256 -addtrust clientAuth
```

The following lines show sample output generated by the previous command. The values shown after subject will be different in your configuration because you entered your own values when you generated the certificate signing request that was saved in the `board001.csr` file:

```
Signature ok
subject=/C=US/ST=CALIFORNIA/L=SANTA MONICA/O=MQTT BOARD 001/OU=MQTT BOARD
001/CN=MQTT BOARD 001/emailAddress=mttboard001@example.com
Getting CA Private Key
```

Run the following command to display data and details for the generated server certificate file:

```
openssl x509 -in board001.crt -noout -text
```

The following lines show sample output that displays details about the signature algorithms, the issuer, the validity and the subject:

```
Certificate:
    Data:
        Version: 1 (0x0)
        Serial Number:
            dd:34:7a:3c:a6:cd:c1:94
        Signature Algorithm: sha256WithRSAEncryption
        Issuer: C=US, ST=CALIFORNIA, L=SAN FRANCISCO, O=CERTIFICATE
        AUTHORITY, CN=CERTIFICATE
        AUTHORITY/emailAddress=CERTIFICATE@EXAMPLE.COM
        Validity
            Not Before: Mar 23 22:10:05 2018 GMT
            Not After : Mar 20 22:10:05 2028 GMT
        Subject: C=US, ST=CALIFORNIA, L=SANTA MONICA, O=MQTT BOARD 001,
        OU=MQTT BOARD 001, CN=MQTT BOARD
        001/emailAddress=mttboard001@example.com
        Subject Public Key Info:
            Public Key Algorithm: rsaEncryption
            RSA Public Key: (2048 bit)
                Modulus (2048 bit):
                    00:d0:9c:dd:9f:3e:db:3f:15:9c:23:40:12:5f:4e:
                    56:2a:30:34:df:88:51:d7:ca:61:bb:99:b5:ab:b4:
                    a6:61:e9:f1:ed:2e:c3:61:7a:f2:0b:70:5b:24:7a:
                    12:3f:cb:5d:76:f7:10:b2:08:24:94:31:0d:80:35:
                    78:2c:19:70:8b:c0:fe:c1:cb:b2:13:5e:9a:d3:68:
                    5d:4d:78:47:5a:a3:d5:63:cd:3c:2f:8b:b1:48:4d:
                    12:11:0b:02:17:f3:4c:56:91:67:9f:98:3d:90:1f:
                    47:09:c0:1b:3a:04:09:2f:b9:fe:f1:e9:df:38:35:
                    f8:12:ee:59:96:b1:ca:57:90:53:19:2b:4f:d3:45:
                    9e:f2:6a:09:95:46:f9:68:6b:c6:4e:89:33:78:4f:
```

```
                        0f:5b:2f:d3:00:d0:12:d7:ca:92:df:f4:86:6e:22:
                        9d:63:a2:f7:de:09:f4:8c:02:ad:03:9c:13:7b:b4:
                        9e:03:d6:99:f4:c0:3f:3f:c3:31:52:12:f1:66:cd:
                        22:5d:48:fb:7f:ca:ac:84:cf:24:c5:c4:85:af:61:
                        de:59:84:a8:e0:fd:ce:44:5d:f2:85:c0:5d:f2:c5:
                        ec:71:04:2c:83:94:cd:71:a1:14:1b:f7:e4:1b:b4:
                        2f:12:70:cb:b7:17:9e:db:c9:23:d1:56:bd:f5:02:
                        c8:3b
                 Exponent: 65537 (0x10001)
          Signature Algorithm: sha256WithRSAEncryption
          55:6a:69:0f:3a:e5:6f:d4:16:0a:4f:67:46:ec:36:ea:a4:54:
          db:04:86:e9:48:ed:0e:83:52:56:75:65:f0:85:34:32:75:0a:
          0a:15:13:73:21:a4:a9:9c:89:b4:73:15:06:2a:b3:e8:ab:7b:
          f4:16:37:17:a9:0e:eb:74:1d:78:c8:df:5e:5f:41:af:53:ca:
          a1:94:d8:d2:f5:87:a5:a9:8a:6a:d1:0e:e0:b7:30:92:d2:94:
          98:65:4c:bf:f9:a7:60:f8:c2:df:7c:4e:28:3c:02:f0:d4:a8:
          f7:16:d5:38:88:43:e4:c4:2e:02:72:ee:4b:6f:cd:2a:d7:3b:
          c4:e8:f4:7d:0e:3b:9b:5b:20:00:69:75:76:ce:79:a1:ed:25:
          f7:f1:3c:96:f8:7d:35:dd:5c:f8:4d:d2:04:32:bb:41:b2:3d:
          1a:5d:f6:63:ff:63:48:ec:85:c2:b3:9c:02:d3:ad:17:59:46:
          3e:10:6f:82:2f:d8:ef:6c:a5:42:3f:55:74:bb:f6:17:59:a0:
          39:e5:16:55:a3:f9:5a:b5:04:c0:61:2a:55:32:56:c2:12:0a:
          2c:c8:8a:23:b1:60:d5:a3:93:f3:a0:e4:e0:a8:98:3b:e1:83:
          ea:43:06:bc:d0:96:0b:c2:0b:95:6b:ce:39:02:7f:19:01:ea:
          47:83:25:c5
Trusted Uses:
TLS Web Client Authentication
No Rejected Uses.
```

After running the previous commands, we will have the following three new files in the certificates directory:

- `board001.key`: Client key
- `board001.csr`: Client certificate signing request
- `board001.crt`: Client certificate file

 The client certificate file is in the PEM format, as are the certificate authority certificate file and the server certificate file.

We will have to provide the following three files to any device that we want to connect to the Mosquitto server:

- `ca.crt`
- `board001.crt`
- `board001.key`

> Never provide additional files to devices that have to establish a connection with the MQTT server. You don't want the devices to be able to generate additional certificates. You just want them to authenticate with a valid certificate.

The `openssl` utility allows us to provide values for many parameters with additional command-line options. Hence, it is possible to automate many of the previous steps to make it easier to generate multiple device certificates.

Configuring TLS client certificate authentication in Mosquitto

Now, we will configure Mosquitto to use TLS client certificate authentication. This way, any client will require the `ca.crt` file and a client certificate, such as the recently generated `board001.crt` file, to establish a communication with the Mosquitto server.

If you are running the Mosquitto server in a Terminal window in macOS or Linux, press *Ctrl* + *C* to stop it. In Windows, stop the appropriate service.

Go to the Mosquitto installation directory and open the `mosquitto.conf` configuration file.

In macOS, Linux, or Windows, add the following line at the end of the configuration file:

```
require_certificate true
```

We specified the `true` value for the `require_certificate` option to make Mosquitto require a valid client certificate for any client that requests a connection to Mosquitto.

Save the changes to the `mosquitto.conf` configuration file and launch Mosquitto again. We will use the `mosquitto_sub` command-line utility included in Mosquitto to generate a simple MQTT client that subscribes to a topic filter and prints all the messages it receives.

Testing the MQTT TLS client authentication with command-line tools

Now, we will use the Mosquitto command-line tools to test the client authentication configuration.

The following command specifies the certificate authority certificate file, the client certificate, and the client key. You have to replace ca.crt, board001.crt, and board001.key with the full path to these files created in the certificates directory. However, it is a better idea to copy these files to a new directory as if we were working with files that will be only available to the device that wants to establish a connection with Mosquitto. As with previous commands, this command uses the -h option followed by the MQTT server host. In this case, we specify the IPv4 address of the computer that is running the Mosquitto MQTT server: 192.168.1.1. Notice that this value must match the IPv4 or IPv6 address that we specified as the value in the **Common Name** field when we generated the server.csr file, that is, the server certificate signing request. If you used a host name as the value in the **Common Name** field instead of an IPv4 or IPv6 address, you will have to use the same host name. The mosquitto_sub utility will create an MQTT subscriber that will establish an encrypted connection with Mosquitto and will provide the client certificate and client key to perform authentication:

```
mosquitto_sub -h 192.168.1.1 -V mqttv311 -p 8883 --cafile ca.crt --cert
board001.crt --key board001.key -t sensors/+/altitude -d
```

With a similar syntax, we will use the mosquitto_pub command-line utility included in Mosquitto to generate a simple MQTT client that publishes a message to a topic that will match the previously specified topic filter, with an encrypted connection and client authentication. Open a Terminal in macOS or Linux, or a Command Prompt in Windows, go to the directory in which Mosquitto is installed, and run the following command. Remember to replace ca.crt, board001.crt, and board001.key with the full path to these files created in the mqtt_certificates directory. In addition, replace 192.168.1.1 with the IPv4 or IPv6 address that we specified as the value in the **Common Name** field when we generated the server.csr file, that is, the server certificate signing request. If you used a host name as the value in the **Common Name** field instead of an IPv4 or IPv6 address, you will have to use the same host name:

```
mosquitto_pub -h 192.168.1.1 -V mqttv311 -p 8883 --cafile ca.crt --cert
board001.crt --key board001.key -t sensors/quadcopter12/altitude -m "361 f"
-d
```

Sometimes, it is necessary to invalidate a client certificate. Mosquitto allows us to specify a PEM-encoded certificate revocation list file. We have to specify the path to this file as a value for the `crlfile` option in the Mosquitto configuration file.

Testing the MQTT TLS configuration with GUI tools

Now, we will use the MQTT.fx GUI utility to generate another MQTT client that uses an encrypted connection and TLS client authentication to publish messages to a topic that matches the topic filter we used for the subscription, `sensors/hexacopter25/altitude`. We have to make changes to the connection options we used when we enabled TLS. We have to specify the client certificate and client key files. Follow these steps:

1. Launch MQTT.fx and click **Disconnect** if you were connected to the Mosquitto MQTT server.
2. Select **local mosquitto** in the drop-down located in the upper-left corner and click on the configuration icon at the right-hand side of this drop-down and at the left-hand side of the **Connect** button. MQTT.fx will display the **Edit Connection Profiles** dialog box with different options for the connection profile named **local mosquitto**.
3. Go to the **Broker Address** textbox and enter the IPv4 or IPv6 address that we specified as the value in the **Common Name** field when we generated the `server.csr` file, that is, the server certificate signing request. If you used a host name as the value in the **Common Name** field instead of an IPv4 or IPv6 address, you will have to use the same host name. If there is no match between the value specified in **Broker Address** and the value indicated in the **Common Name** field, the Mosquitto server will reject the client.
4. Click the **SSL/TLS** button.
5. Make sure the **Enable SSL/TLS** checkbox is activated.
6. Activate the **Self signed certificates** radio button.
7. Enter or select the full path to the `ca.crt` file that you created in the `mqtt_certificates` folder in the **CA File** textbox.
8. Enter or select the full path to the `board001.crt` file that you created in the `mqtt_ertificates` folder in the **Client Certificate File** textbox.

9. Enter or select the full path to the `board001.key` file that you created in the `mqtt_certificates` folder in the **Client Key File** textbox.

10. Make sure the **PEM Formatted** checkbox is activated. The following screenshot shows a dialog box with the selected options and sample values for the different textboxes:

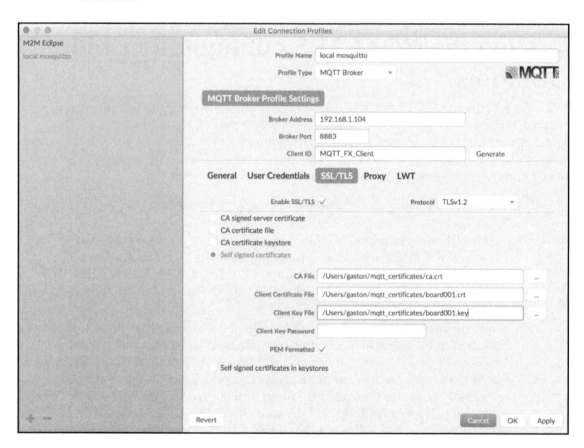

11. Click **OK**. Then, click on the **Connect** button. MQTT.fx will establish an encrypted connection with the local Mosquitto server by using the certificate and key files we have specified. Notice that the **Connect** button is disabled and the **Disconnect** button is enabled because the client is connected to the Mosquitto server.

12. Click **Subscribe** and enter `sensors/+/altitude` in the drop-down at the left-hand side of the **Subscribe** button. Then, click the **Subscribe** button. MQTT.fx will display a new panel at the left-hand side with the topic filter to which we have subscribed.

13. Click **Publish** and enter `sensors/hexacopter25/altitude` in the drop-down at the left-hand side of the **Publish** button.

14. Enter the following text in the textbox below the Publish button: `1153 f`.

15. Then, click the **Publish** button. MQTT.fx will publish the entered text to the specified topic.

16. Click **Subscribe** and you will see the published message, as shown in the following screenshot:

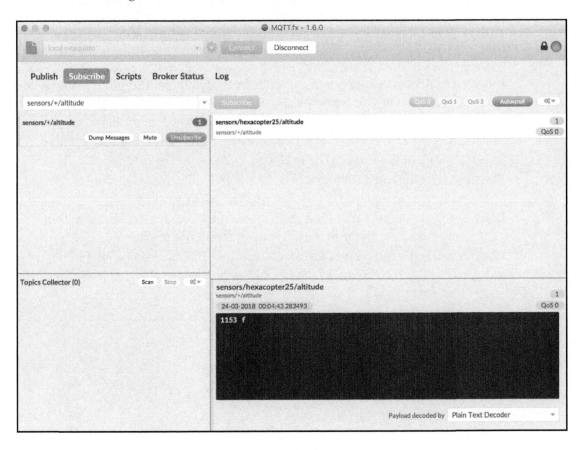

Now, we will use the MQTT-spy GUI utility to generate another MQTT client that uses an encrypted connection to publish messages to another topic that will match the sensors/+/altitude topic filter: sensors/quadcopter500/altitude. Follow these steps:

1. Launch MQTT-spy.
2. Select **Connections** | **New connection** or **Connections** | **Manage** connections if you were already running MQTT-spy or saved the previous settings. The **Connection list** dialog box will appear.
3. Click on the **Connectivity** tab and make sure MQTT 3.1.1 is selected in the **Protocol version** drop-down.
4. Go to the **Server URI(s)** textbox and enter the IPv4 or IPv6 address that we specified as the value in the **Common Name** field when we generated the server.csr file, that is, the server certificate signing request. If you used a host name as the value in the **Common Name** field instead of an IPv4 or IPv6 address, you will have to use the same host name. If there is no match between the value specified in **Broker Address** and the value indicated in the **Common Name** field, the Mosquitto server will reject the client generated by the MQTT-spy utility.
5. Click on the **Security** tab and on the **TLS** tab below the **User auth.** tab.
6. Select **CA certificate & client certificate/key** in the **TLS/SSL mode** drop-down.
7. Select **TLSv1.2** in the **Protocol** drop-down.
8. Enter or select the full path to the ca.crt file that you created in the mqtt_certificates folder in the **CA certificate file** textbox.
9. Enter or select the full path to the board001.crt file that you created in the mqtt_ertificates folder in the **Client certificate file** textbox.
10. Enter or select the full path to the board001.key file that you created in the mqtt_certificates folder in the **Client key file** textbox.

11. Activate the **Client key in PEM format** checkbox. Finally, click **Open connection** or **Close and re-open existing connection**. The following screenshot shows a dialog box with the selected options and sample values for the textboxes:

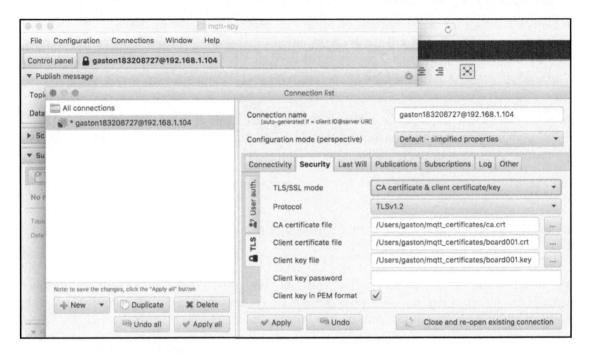

12. MQTT-spy will close the dialog box and will display a new tab with a green background and the connection name that appeared highlighted and selected at the left-hand side in the **Connection list** dialog box. Make sure you click on the tab for the new connection.

13. Enter `sensors/quadcopter500/altitude` in the **Topic** drop-down.

14. Enter the following text in the **Data** textbox: `1417 f`.

15. Click the **Publish** button. MQTT-spy will publish the entered text to the specified topic and you will be able to see the message in both the MQTT.fx subscriber and the `mosquitto-sub` subscriber.

As happens with any security configuration, any checkbox that isn't activated based on the previous instructions won't allow the MQTT client to establish a connection with Mosquitto. It is very important to remember that the certificates use the PEM format.

Forcing the TLS protocol version to a specific number

It is good practice to use the highest possible TLS protocol version. By default, a Mosquitto server accepts TLS 1.0, 1.1, and 1.2. If all the clients are capable of working with the highest TLS protocol version supported by Mosquitto, we should force Mosquitto to use only the highest version. This way, we make sure that we won't be vulnerable to attacks on previous TLS versions.

Now, we will make the necessary changes in the configuration file to force the use of TLS 1.2. If you are running the Mosquitto server in a Terminal window in macOS or Linux, press *Ctrl + C* to stop it. In Windows, stop the appropriate service.

Go to the Mosquitto installation directory and open the `mosquitto.conf` configuration file.

In macOS, Linux, or Windows, add the following line at the end of the configuration file:

```
tls_version tlsv1.2
```

We specified the `tlsv1.2` value for the `tls_version` option to make Mosquitto work only with TLS 1.2. Any client that uses a previous TLS version won't be able to establish a connection with the Mosquitto server.

Save the changes to the `mosquitto.conf` configuration file and launch Mosquitto again. We specified the TLS version when we configured the connection in both the MQTT.fx and MQTT-spy GUI utilities; specifically, we specified TLS 1.2 as the desired TLS version for the client, and therefore no additional changes are required. We must use the `--tls-version tlsv1.2` option in the `mosquitto_sub` and `mosquitto_pub` command-line utilities.

Open a Terminal in macOS or Linux, or a Command Prompt in Windows, go to the directory in which Mosquitto is installed, and run the following command. Remember to use the full paths for the `ca.crt`, `device.001`, and `device.key` files. In addition, replace `192.168.1.1` with the IPv4 or IPv6 address that we specified as the value in the **Common Name** field when we generated the `server.csr` file, that is, the server certificate signing request. If you used a host name as the value in the **Common Name** field instead of an IPv4 or IPv6 address, you will have to use the same host name:

```
mosquitto_pub -h 192.168.1.1 --tls-version tlsv1.2 -V mqttv311 -p 8883 --
cafile ca.crt -t sensors/octocopter01/altitude -m "1025 f" -d
```

The previous command specified the use of TLS 1.2, and therefore the MQTT client can establish a connection with the Mosquitto server and publish the message. If we specify a different TLS version, the `mosquitto_pub` command won't be able to connect with the Mosquitto server.

Test your knowledge

Let's see whether you can answer the following questions correctly:

1. Which is the default port number for MQTT over TLS:
    1. `1883`
    2. `5883`
    3. `8883`

2. Which of the following utilities allows us to generate an X.509 digital certificate:
    1. OpenX509
    2. TLS4Devs
    3. OpenSSL

3. When we use MQTT over TLS:
    1. There are both bandwidth and processing overheads compared to MQTT over TCP without TLS
    2. There is just a small bandwith overhead but no processing overhead at all compared to MQTT over TCP without TLS
    3. There is no overhead compared to MQTT over TCP without TLS

4. Which of the following can we use to secure and encrypt communications between the MQTT clients and the MQTT server:
    1. TCPS
    2. TLS
    3. HTTPS

5. If we specify `true` as the value for the `require_certificate` option of the Mosquitto configuration file (`mosquitto.conf`):
    1. Clients that want to connect to the MQTT server will require a client certificate
    2. Clients that want to connect to the MQTT server won't require a client certificate
    3. Clients that want to connect to the MQTT server can provide an optional client certificate

The rights answers are included in the `Appendix`, *Solutions*.

Summary

In this chapter, we generated a private certificate authority, a server certificate, and client certificates to enable TLS transport security and TLS client authentication with Mosquitto. Communications between MQTT clients and the MQTT server are encrypted.

We worked with OpenSSL to generate self-signed digital certificates for our development environment. We tested the MQTT TLS configuration with MQTT.fx, MQTT-spy, and Mosquitto command-line utilities. We forced Mosquitto to use only a specific TLS version.

There are many other security topics related to MQTT servers and Mosquitto. We will work with some of them in forthcoming chapters, in which we will develop applications that will use MQTT with Python.

Now that we understand how to encrypt communications between MQTT clients and the Mosquitto server, we will understand MQTT libraries and we will write Python code to control a vehicle with MQTT messages delivered through encrypted connections, which are the topics that we are going to discuss in `Chapter 4`, *Writing Code to Control a Vehicle with Python and MQTT Messages*.

4
Writing Code to Control a Vehicle with Python and MQTT Messages

In this chapter, we will write Python 3.x code to control a vehicle with MQTT messages delivered through encrypted connections (TLS 1.2). We will write code that will be able to run on different popular IoT platforms, such as a Raspberry Pi 3 board. We will understand how we can leverage our knowledge of the MQTT protocol to build a solution based on requirements. We will learn to work with the latest version of the Eclipse Paho MQTT Python client library. We will gain take an in-depth look at the following:

- Understanding the requirements to control a vehicle with MQTT
- Defining the topics and commands
- Learning the benefits of working with Python
- Creating a virtual environment with Python 3.x and PEP 405
- Understanding the directory structure for a virtual environment
- Activating the virtual environment
- Deactivating the virtual environment
- Installing paho-mqtt for Python
- Connecting a client to the secured MQTT server with paho-mqtt
- Understanding callbacks
- Subscribing to topics with Python
- Configuring certificates for IoT boards that will work as clients
- Creating a class to represent a vehicle
- Receiving messages in Python
- Working with multiple calls to the loop method

Understanding the requirements to control a vehicle with MQTT

In the previous three chapters, we learned how MQTT works in detail. We understood how to establish a connection between an MQTT client and an MQTT server. We learned what happened when we subscribed to topic filters and when a publisher sent messages to specific topics. We installed a Mosquitto server and then we secured it.

Now, we will use Python as our main programming language to generate MQTT clients that will act as publishers and subscribers. We will connect a Python MQTT client to the MQTT server and we will process commands to control a small vehicle with MQTT messages. The small vehicle replicates many capabilities found in real-life road vehicles.

We will use TLS encryption and TLS authentication because we don't want any MQTT client to be able to send commands to our vehicle. We want our Python 3.x code to run on many platforms because we will use the same code base to control vehicles that use the following IoT boards:

- Raspberry Pi 3 Model B+
- Qualcomm DragonBoard 410c
- BeagleBone Black
- MinnowBoard Turbot Quad-Core
- LattePanda 2G
- UP Core 4GB
- UP Squared

Depending on the platform, each vehicle is going to provide additional features because some boards are more powerful compared to other boards. However, we will focus on the basic features to keep our example simple and stay concentrated on MQTT. Then, we will be able to use this project as a baseline for other solutions that require us to run code on an IoT board that runs Python 3.x code, has to connect to an MQTT server, and processes commands.

The code that runs on the boards that power the vehicles must be able to process commands received in messages on a specific topic. We will use JSON strings in the payloads.

A client application also written in Python must be able to control one or more vehicles. We will also write the client application in Python and it will publish MQTT messages with JSON strings to the topic for each vehicle. The client application must display the results of executing each command. Each vehicle must publish a message to a specific topic whenever a command is successfully executed.

Defining the topics and commands

We will use the following topic name to publish the commands for a vehicle: `vehicles/vehiclename/commands`, where `vehiclename` must be replaced with a unique name assigned to a vehicle. For example, if we assign `vehiclepi01` as the name for a vehicle that is powered by a Raspberry Pi 3 Model B+ board, we will have to publish commands to the `vehicles/vehiclepi01/commands` topic. The Python code that runs on this board will subscribe to this topic to receive messages with commands and react to them.

We will use the following topic name to make the vehicles publish details about the successfully executed commands: `vehicles/vehiclename/executedcommands`, where `vehiclename` must be replaced with a unique name assigned to a vehicle. For example, if we assign `vehiclebeagle03` as the name for a vehicle that is powered by a BeagleBone Black board, the client that wants to receive information about successfully processed commands has to subscribe to the `vehicles/vehiclebeagle03/executedcommands` topic.

The commands will be sent in a JSON string with a key-value pair. The key must be equal to CMD and the value must specify any of the following valid commands. When the command requires additional parameters, the parameter name must be included in the next key and the value for this parameter in the value for this key:

- `TURN_ON_ENGINE`: Turn on the vehicle's engine.
- `TURN_OFF_ENGINE`: Turn off the vehicle's engine.
- `LOCK_DOORS`: Close and lock the vehicle's doors.

- UNLOCK_DOORS: Unlock and open the vehicle's doors.
- PARK: Park the vehicle.
- PARK_IN_SAFE_PLACE: Park the vehicle in a safe place that is configured for the vehicle.
- TURN_ON_HEADLIGHTS: Turn on the vehicle's headlights.
- TURN_OFF_HEADLIGHTS: Turn off the vehicle's headlights.
- TURN_ON_PARKING_LIGHTS: Turn on the vehicle's parking lights, also known as sidelights.
- TURN_OFF_PARKING_LIGHTS: Turn off the vehicle's parking lights, also known as sidelights.
- ACCELERATE: Accelerate the vehicle, that is, press the gas pedal.
- BRAKE: Brake the vehicle, that is, press the brake pedal.
- ROTATE_RIGHT: Make the vehicle rotate to the right. We must specify how many degrees we want the vehicle to rotate right in the value for the DEGREES key.
- ROTATE_LEFT: Make the vehicle rotate to the left. We must specify how many degrees we want the vehicle to rotate left in the value for the DEGREES key.
- SET_MAX_SPEED: Set the maximum speed that we allow to the vehicle. We must specify the desired maximum speed in miles per hour in the value for the MPH key.
- SET_MIN_SPEED: Set the minimum speed that we allow to the vehicle. We must specify the desired minimum speed in miles per hour in the value for the MPH key.

The following line shows an example of the payload for the command that turns on the vehicle's engine:

```
{"CMD": "TURN_ON_ENGINE"}
```

The following line shows an example of the payload for the command that sets the maximum speed for the vehicle to five miles per hour:

```
{"CMD": "SET_MAX_SPEED", "MPH": 5}
```

We have all the necessary details to start coding with Python.

Creating a virtual environment with Python 3.6.x and PEP 405

In the next sections and chapters, we will be writing different pieces of Python code that will subscribe to topics and will also publish messages to topics. As happens whenever we want to isolate an environment that requires additional packages, it is convenient to work with Python virtual environments. Python 3.3 introduced lightweight virtual environments, and they were improved in Python 3.4. We will work with these virtual environments, and therefore, you will need Python 3.4 or greater. You can read more about PEP 405 Python Virtual Environment, which introduced the `venv` module, here: `https://www.python.org/dev/peps/pep-0405`.

All the examples for this book were tested on Python 3.6.2 on macOS and Linux. The examples were also tested on the IoT boards mentioned throughout the book and their most popular operating systems. For example, all the examples were tested on Raspbian. Raspbian is based on Debian Linux, and therefore, all the instructions for Linux will work for Raspbian.

If you decide to use the popular `virtualenv` (`https://pypi.python.org/pypi/virtualenv`) third-party virtual environment builder or the virtual environment options provided by your Python IDE, you just have to make sure that you activate your virtual environment with the appropriate mechanism whenever it is necessary to do so, instead of following the step explained to activate the virtual environment generated with the `venv` module integrated in Python.

Each virtual environment we create with `venv` is an isolated environment and it will have its own independent set of installed Python packages in its site directories (folders). When we create a virtual environment with `venv` in Python 3.4 and greater, `pip` is included in the new virtual environment. In Python 3.3, it was necessary to manually install `pip` after creating the virtual environment. Note that the instructions provided are compatible with Python 3.4 or greater, including Python 3.6.x. The following commands assume that you have Python 3.5.x or greater installed on Linux, macOS, or Windows.

First, we have to select the target folder or directory for our lightweight virtual environment. The following is the path we will use in the example for Linux and macOS. The target folder for the virtual environment will be the `HillarMQTT/01` folder within our home directory. For example, if our home directory in macOS or Linux is `/Users/gaston`, the virtual environment will be created within `/Users/gaston/HillarMQTT/01`. You can replace the specified path with your desired path in each command:

```
~/HillarMQTT/01
```

The following is the path we will use in the example for Windows. The target folder for the virtual environment will be the `HillarMQTT\01` folder within our user profile folder. For example, if our user profile folder is `C:\Users\gaston`, the virtual environment will be created within `C:\Users\gaston\HillarMQTT\01`. You can replace the specified path with your desired path in each command:

```
%USERPROFILE%\HillarMQTT\01
```

In Windows PowerShell, the previous path would be:

```
$env:userprofile\HillarMQTT\01
```

Now, we have to use the `-m` option followed by the `venv` module name and the desired path to make Python run this module as a script and create a virtual environment in the specified path. The instructions are different depending on the platform in which we are creating the virtual environment.

Open Terminal in Linux or macOS and execute the following command to create a virtual environment:

```
python3 -m venv ~/HillarMQTT/01
```

In Windows, in Command Prompt, execute the following command to create a virtual environment:

```
python -m venv %USERPROFILE%\HillarMQTT\01
```

If you want to work with Windows PowerShell, execute the following command to create a virtual environment:

```
python -m venv $env:userprofile\HillarMQTT\01
```

None of the previous commands produce any output. The script created the specified target folder and installed `pip` by invoking `ensurepip` because we didn't specify the `--without-pip` option.

Understanding the directory structure for a virtual environment

The specified target folder has a new directory tree that contains Python-executable files and other files that indicate it is a PEP405 virtual environment.

In the root directory for the virtual environment, the `pyenv.cfg` configuration file specifies different options for the virtual environment and its existence is an indicator that we are in the root folder for a virtual environment. In Linux and macOS, the folder will have the following main subfolders: `bin`, `include`, `lib`, `lib/python3.6`, and `lib/python3.6/site-packages`. Note that the folder names can be different based on the specific Python version. In Windows, the folder will have the following main subfolders: `Include`, `Lib`, `Lib\site-packages`, and `Scripts`. The directory trees for the virtual environment in each platform are the same as the layout of the Python installation in these platforms.

The following screenshot shows the folders and files in the directory trees generated for the `01` virtual environment in macOS and Linux platforms:

The following screenshot shows the main folders in the directory trees generated for the virtual environment in Windows:

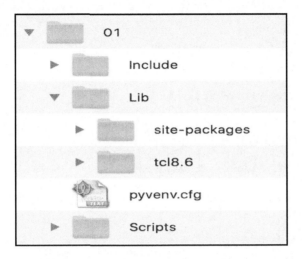

After we activate the virtual environment, we will install third-party packages into the virtual environment and the modules will be located within the `lib/python3.6/site-packages` or `Lib\site-packages` folder, based on the platform and the specific Python version. The executables will be copied to the `bin` or `Scripts` folder, based on the platform. The packages we install won't make changes to other virtual environments or our base Python environment.

Activating the virtual environment

Now that we have created a virtual environment, we will run a platform-specific script to activate it. After we activate the virtual environment, we will install packages that will only be available in this virtual environment. This way, we will work with an isolated environment in which all the packages we install won't affect our main Python environment.

Run the following command in Terminal in Linux or macOS. Note that the results of this command will be accurate if you don't start a different shell than the default shell in the Terminal session. If you have doubts, check your Terminal configuration and preferences:

```
echo $SHELL
```

The command will display the name of the shell you are using in Terminal. In macOS, the default is `/bin/bash` and this means you are working with the bash shell. Depending on the shell, you must run a different command to activate the virtual environment in Linux or macOS.

If your Terminal is configured to use the bash shell in Linux or macOS, run the following command to activate the virtual environment. The command also works for the `zsh` shell:

```
source ~/HillarMQTT/01/bin/activate
```

If your Terminal is configured to use either the `csh` or `tcsh` shell, run the following command to activate the virtual environment:

```
source ~/HillarMQTT/01/bin/activate.csh
```

If your Terminal is configured to use the `fish` shell, run the following command to activate the virtual environment:

```
source ~/HillarMQTT/01/bin/activate.fish
```

After you activate the virtual environment, the Command Prompt will display the virtual environment root folder name enclosed in parentheses as a prefix of the default prompt to remind us that we are working in the virtual environment. In this case, we will see **(01)** as a prefix for the Command Prompt because the root folder for the activated virtual environment is `01`.

The following screenshot shows the virtual environment activated in a macOS High Sierra Terminal with a `bash` shell, after executing the previously shown commands:

```
⬤ ⬤ ⬤                          ↑ gaston — -bash — 80×24
Gastons-MacBook-Pro:~ gaston$ python3 -m venv ~/HillarMQTT/010
Gastons-MacBook-Pro:~ gaston$ echo $SHELL
/bin/bash
Gastons-MacBook-Pro:~ gaston$ source ~/HillarMQTT/01/bin/activate
(01) Gastons-MacBook-Pro:~ gaston$ ▊
```

As we can see from the previous screenshot, the prompt changed from `Gastons-MacBook-Pro:~ gaston$` to `(01) Gastons-MacBook-Pro:~ gaston$` after the activation of the virtual environment.

In Windows, you can run either a batch file in Command Prompt or a Windows PowerShell script to activate the virtual environment.

If you prefer Command Prompt, run the following command in the Windows command line to activate the virtual environment:

```
%USERPROFILE%\HillarMQTT\01\Scripts\activate.bat
```

The following screenshot shows the virtual environment activated in a Windows 10 Command Prompt, after executing the previously shown commands:

As we can see from the previous screenshot, the prompt changed from `C:\Users\gaston` to `(01) C:\Users\gaston` after the activation of the virtual environment.

If you prefer Windows PowerShell, launch it and run the following commands to activate the virtual environment. Note that you must have scripts execution enabled in Windows PowerShell to be able to run the script:

```
cd $env:USERPROFILE
.\HillarMQTT\01\Scripts\Activate.ps1
```

If you receive an error similar to the following, it means that you don't have scripts execution enabled:

```
C:\Users\gaston\HillarMQTT\01\Scripts\Activate.ps1 : File
C:\Users\gaston\HillarMQTT\01\Scripts\Activate.ps1 cannot be loaded because
running scripts is disabled on this system. For more information, see
about_Execution_Policies at
http://go.microsoft.com/fwlink/?LinkID=135170.
At line:1 char:1
+ C:\Users\gaston\HillarMQTT\01\Scripts\Activate.ps1
+ ~~~~~~~~~~~~~~~~~~~~~~~~~~~~~~~~~~~~~~~~~~~~~~~~~~~~
  + CategoryInfo : SecurityError: (:) [], PSSecurityException
  + FullyQualifiedErrorId : UnauthorizedAccess
```

The Windows PowerShell default execution policy is `Restricted`. This policy allows the execution of individual commands but it doesn't run scripts. Thus, if you want to work with Windows PowerShell, you will have to change the policy to allow the execution of scripts. It is very important to make sure that you understand the risks of the Windows PowerShell execution policies that allow you to run unsigned scripts. For more information about the different policies, check the following web page: `https://docs.microsoft.com/` `en-us/powershell/module/microsoft.powershell.core/about/about_execution_` `policies?view=powershell-6`.

The following screenshot shows the virtual environment activated in a Windows 10 PowerShell, after executing the previously shown commands:

```
Windows PowerShell
Windows PowerShell
Copyright (C) Microsoft Corporation. All rights reserved.

PS C:\Users\gaston> python -m venv $env:userprofile\HillarMQTT\01
PS C:\Users\gaston> cd $env:USERPROFILE
PS C:\Users\gaston> .\HillarMQTT\01\Scripts\Activate.ps1
(01) PS C:\Users\gaston>
```

Deactivating the virtual environment

It is extremely easy to deactivate a virtual environment generated with the previously explained process. The deactivation will remove all the changes made in the environment variables and will change the prompt back to its default message. Once you deactivate a virtual environment, you will go back to the default Python environment.

In macOS or Linux, just type `deactivate` and press *Enter*.

In Command Prompt, you have to run the `deactivate.bat` batch file included in the `Scripts` folder. In our example, the full path for this file is `%USERPROFILE%\HillarMQTT\01\Scripts\deactivate.bat`.

In Windows PowerShell, you have to run the `Deactivate.ps1` script in the `Scripts` folder. In our example, the full path for this file is `$env:userprofile\HillarMQTT\01\Scripts\Deactivate.ps1`. Remember that you must have scripts execution enabled in Windows PowerShell to be able to run the script.

The instructions in the next sections assume that the virtual environment we have created is activated.

Installing paho-mqtt for Python

The Eclipse Paho project provides an open source client implementation of MQTT. The project includes a Python client, also known as the Paho Python Client or Eclipse Paho MQTT Python client library. This Python client has been contributed from the Mosquitto project and was originally known as the Mosquitto Python client. The following is the web page for the Eclipse Paho project: http://www.eclipse.org/paho. The following is the web page for the Eclipse Paho MQTT Python client library version 1.3.1, that is, the paho-mqtt module version 1.3.1: https://pypi.python.org/pypi/paho-mqtt/1.3.1.

We can use paho-mqtt in many modern IoT boards that support Python 3.x or greater. We just need to make sure that pip is installed to make it easier to install paho-mqtt. You can use your development computer to run the examples or any of the afore mentioned boards.

Make sure that the virtual environment we created in the previous steps is activated before moving forward with the next steps.

If you are going to work with an IoT board to run the example, make sure that you run all the commands in the SSH terminal or the Terminal window that runs on the board. If you use your development computer, run the commands in a Terminal in macOS or Linux, or Command Prompt in Windows.

Now, we will use pip installer to install paho-mqtt 1.3.1. We just need to run the following command in the SSH terminal or the local terminal window we are using with the board, or on the computer we are using to install the package:

```
pip install paho-mqtt==1.3.1
```

Some IoT boards have operating systems that will require you to install `pip` before running the previous commands. On Raspberry Pi 3 boards with Raspbian, `pip` is already installed. If you are using your computer, the Python installation usually includes `pip`.

If you have Python installed in the default folder in Windows and you aren't working with a Python virtual environment, you will have to run the previous command in an administrator Command Prompt. If you aren't working with a Python virtual environment in Raspbian, you will have to run the previous command with `sudo` as a prefix: `sudo pip install paho-mqtt`. However, as previously explained, it is highly recommended to use a virtual environment.

The last lines for the output will indicate that the `paho-mqtt` package version 1.3.1 has been successfully installed. The output will be similar to the following lines, but not exactly the same because it will vary based on the platform in which you are running the command:

```
Collecting paho-mqtt==1.3.1
  Downloading paho-mqtt-1.3.1.tar.gz (80kB)
  100% |###############################| 81kB 1.2MB/s
Installing collected packages: paho-mqtt
  Running setup.py install for paho-mqtt ... done
Successfully installed paho-mqtt-1.3.1
```

Connecting a client to the secured MQTT server with paho-mqtt

First, we will use `paho-mqtt` to create an MQTT client that connects to the Mosquitto MQTT server. We will write a few lines of Python code to establish a secured connection and subscribe to a topic.

In Chapter 3, *Securing an MQTT 3.1.1 Mosquitto Server*, we secured our Mosquitto server, and therefore, we will use the digital certificates we created to authenticate the client. Most of the time, we will work with an MQTT server that uses TLS, and therefore, it is a good idea to learn how to establish a connection with TLS and TLS authentication. It is easier to establish an unsecured connection with an MQTT server, but it won't be the most common scenario we will face when developing applications that work with MQTT.

First, we need to copy the following files, which we created in `Chapter 3`, *Securing an MQTT 3.1.1 Mosquitto Server*, to a directory on the computer or device we will use to run a Python script. We saved the files in a directory called `mqtt_certificates`. Create a `board_certificates` directory on the computer or board you are going to use as the MQTT client for this example. Copy the following three files to this new directory:

- `ca.crt`: Certificate authority certificate file
- `board001.crt`: Client certificate file
- `board001.key`: Client key

Now, we will create a new Python file named `config.py` in the main virtual environment folder. The following lines show the code for this file that defines many configuration values that will be used to establish a connection with the Mosquitto MQTT server. This way, all the configuration values are included in a specific Python script. You have to replace the `/Users/gaston/board_certificates` value in the `certificates_path` string with the path to the `board_certificates` directory you created. In addition, replace the value for the `mqtt_server_host` with the IP address or hostname for the Mosquitto server or any other MQTT server you might decide to use. The code file for the sample is included in the `mqtt_python_gaston_hillar_04_01` folder, in the `config.py` file:

```
import os.path

# Replace /Users/gaston/python_certificates with the path
# in which you saved the certificate authority file,
# the client certificate file and the client key
certificates_path = "/Users/gaston/python_certificates"
ca_certificate = os.path.join(certificates_path, "ca.crt")
client_certificate = os.path.join(certificates_path, "board001.crt")
client_key = os.path.join(certificates_path, "board001.key")
# Replace 192.168.1.101 with the IP or hostname for the Mosquitto
# or other MQTT server
# Make sure the IP or hostname matches the value
# you used for Common Name
mqtt_server_host = "192.168.1.101"
mqtt_server_port = 8883
mqtt_keepalive = 60
```

The code declares the `certificates_path` variable initialized with a string that specifies the path in which you saved the certificate authority file, the client certificate file, and the client key (`ca.crt`, `board001.crt`, and `board001.key`). Then, the code declares the following string variables with the full path to the certificate and key files we need to configure TLS and the TLS client authentication: `ca_certificate`, `client_certificate`, and `client_key`.

> The call to `os.path.join` makes it easy to join the path specified in the `certificates_path` variable with the filename and generate the full path. The `os.path.join` function works for any platform, and therefore, we don't have to worry about whether to use a slash (/) or a backslash (\) to join the path with the filename. Sometimes, we can develop and test in Windows and then run the code on an IoT board that can use different Unix or Linux flavors, such as Raspbian or Ubuntu. The usage of `os.path.join` makes our job easier in scenarios where we switch between different platforms.

The `mqtt_server_host`, `mqtt_server_port`, and `mqtt_keepalive` variables specify the IP address for the MQTT server (the Mosquitto server), the port that we want to use (`8883`), and the number of seconds for the keep alive option. It is very important to replace `192.168.1.101` with the IP address for the MQTT server. We specify `8883` for `mqtt_server_port` because we use TLS and this is the default port for MQTT over TLS, as we learned in Chapter 3, *Securing an MQTT 3.1.1 Mosquitto Server*.

Now, we will create a new Python file named `subscribe_with_paho.py` in the main virtual environment folder. The following lines show the code for this file that establishes a connection with our Mosquitto MQTT server, subscribes to the `vehicles/vehiclepi01/tests` topic filter, and prints all the messages received in the subscribed topic filter. The code file for the sample is included in the `mqtt_python_gaston_hillar_04_01` folder, in the `subscribe_with_paho.py` file:

```
from config import *
import paho.mqtt.client as mqtt


def on_connect(client, userdata, flags, rc):
    print("Result from connect: {}".format(
        mqtt.connack_string(rc)))
    # Subscribe to the vehicles/vehiclepi01/tests topic filter
    client.subscribe("vehicles/vehiclepi01/tests", qos=2)

def on_subscribe(client, userdata, mid, granted_qos):
```

```
        print("I've subscribed with QoS: {}".format(
            granted_qos[0]))

    def on_message(client, userdata, msg):
        print("Message received. Topic: {}. Payload: {}".format(
            msg.topic,
            str(msg.payload)))


    if __name__ == "__main__":
        client = mqtt.Client(protocol=mqtt.MQTTv311)
        client.on_connect = on_connect
        client.on_subscribe = on_subscribe
        client.on_message = on_message
        client.tls_set(ca_certs = ca_certificate,
            certfile=client_certificate,
            keyfile=client_key)
        client.connect(host=mqtt_server_host,
            port=mqtt_server_port,
            keepalive=mqtt_keepalive)
        client.loop_forever()
```

Note that the code is compatible with `paho-mqtt` version 1.3.1. Previous versions of `paho-mqtt` aren't compatible with the code. Hence, make sure you follow the previously explained steps to install `paho-mqtt` version 1.3.1.

Understanding callbacks

The previous code uses the recently installed `paho-mqtt` version 1.3.1 module to establish an encrypted connection with the MQTT server, subscribe to the `vehicles/vehiclepi01/tests` topic filter, and run code when we receive messages in the topic. We will use this code to understand the basics of `paho-mqtt`. The code is a very simple version of an MQTT client that subscribes to a topic filter and we will definitely improve it in the next sections.

The first line imports the variables we have declared in the previously coded `config.py` file. The second line imports `paho.mqtt.client` as `mqtt`. This way, whenever we use the `mqtt` alias, we will be referencing `paho.mqtt.client`.

When we declare a function, we pass this function as an argument to another function or method, or we assign this function to an attribute and then some code calls this function at some time; this mechanism is known as a **callback.** The name callback is used because the code calls back a function at some time. The `paho-mqtt` version 1.3.1 package requires us to work with many callbacks, and therefore, it is very important to understand how they work.

The code declares the following three functions that we specify as callbacks later:

- `on_connect`: This function will be called when the MQTT client receives a CONNACK response from the MQTT server, that is, when a connection has been successfully established with the MQTT server.
- `on_subscribe`: This function will be called when the MQTT client receives a SUBACK response from the MQTT server, that is, when a subscription has been successfully completed.
- `on_message`: This function will be called when the MQTT client receives a PUBLISH message from the MQTT server. Whenever the MQTT server publishes a message based on the subscriptions for the client, this function will be called.

The next table summarizes the functions that will be called based on the received responses from the MQTT server:

Response from the MQTT server	Function that will be called
CONNACK	on_connnect
SUBACK	on_subscribe
PUBLISH	on_message

The code for the main block creates an instance of the `mqtt.Client` class (`paho.mqtt.client.Client`) that represents an MQTT client. We use this instance to communicate with our MQTT server: Mosquitto. If we used the default parameters to create the new instance, we would work with MQTT version 3.1. We want to work with MQTT version 3.11, and therefore, we specified `mqtt.MQTTv311` as the value for the protocol argument.

Then, the code assigns functions to attributes. The following table summarizes these assignments:

Attribute	Assigned function
`client.on_connect`	`on_connect`
`client.on_message`	`on_message`
`client.on_subscribe`	`on_subscribe`

The call to the `client.tls_set` method configures encryption and authentication options. It is very important to call this method before running the `client.connect` method. We specify the full string paths to the certificate authority certificate file, the client certificate, and the client key in the `ca_certs`, `certfile`, and `keyfile` arguments. The `ca_certs` argument name is a bit confusing, but we just need to specify the string path to the certificate authority certificate file, not multiple certificates.

Finally, the main block calls the `client.connect` method and specifies the values for the `host`, `port`, and `keepalive` arguments. This way, the code asks the MQTT client to establish a connection to the specified MQTT server.

The `connect` method runs with an asynchronous execution, and therefore, it is a non-blocking call.

After a connection has been successfully established with the MQTT server, the specified callback in the `client.on_connect` attribute will be executed, that is, the `on_connect` function. This function receives the `mqtt.Client` instance that established the connection with the MQTT server in the client argument.

If you want to establish a connection with an MQTT server that isn't using TLS, you don't need to call the `client.tls_set` method. In addition, you need to use the appropriate port instead of the `8883` port that is specified when working with TLS. Remember that the default port when you don't work with TLS is `1883`.

Subscribing to topics with Python

The code calls the `client.subscribe` method with `"vehicles/vehiclepi01/tests"` as an argument to subscribe to this specific single topic and the `qos` argument set to 2 to request a QoS level of 2.

 In this case, we will only subscribe to one topic. However, it is very important to know that we are not limited to subscribing to a single topic filter; we might subscribe to many topic filters with a single call to the `subscribe` method.

After the MQTT server confirms the successful subscription to the specified topic filter with a SUBACK response, the specified callback in the `client.on_subscribe` attribute will be executed, that is, the `on_subscribe` function. This function receives a list of integers in the `granted_qos` argument that provides the QoS level that the MQTT server has granted for each of the topic filter subscription requests. The code in the `on_subscribe` function displays the QoS level granted by the MQTT server for the topic filter we specified. In this case, we just subscribed to a single topic filter, and therefore, the code grabs the first value from the received `granted_qos` array.

Whenever there is a new message received that matches the topic filter to which we have subscribed, the specified callback in the `client.on_messsage` attribute will be executed, that is, the `on_message` function. This function receives the `mqtt.Client` instance that established the connection with the MQTT server in the client argument and an `mqtt.MQTTMessage` instance in the `msg` argument. The `mqtt.MQTTMessage` class describes an incoming message.

In this case, whenever the `on_message` function is executed, the value in `msg.topic` will always match `"vehicles/vehiclepi01/tests"` because we just subscribed to a single topic and no other topic name will match the topic filter. However, if we subscribed to one or many topic filters to which more than one topic might match, it would always be necessary to check which is the topic in which the message was sent by checking the value of the `msg.topic` attribute.

The code in the `on_message` function prints the topic for the message that has been received, `msg.topic`, and the string representation of the payload for the message, that is, the `msg.payload` attribute.

Finally, the main block calls the `client.loop_forever` method that calls the `loop` method for us in an infinite blocking loop. At this point, we only want to run the MQTT client loop in our program. We will receive the messages whose topic matches the topic to which we have subscribed.

> The `loop` method is responsible for processing the network events, that is, it makes sure communication with the MQTT server is carried out. You can think about the `loop` method as the equivalent of synchronizing your email client to receive incoming messages and send the messages in the outbox.

Make sure the Mosquitto server or any other MQTT server you might want to use for this example is running. Then, execute the following line to start the example on any computer or device that you want to use as the MQTT client and uses Linux or macOS:

```
python3 subscribe_with_paho.py
```

In Windows, you must execute the following line:

```
python subscribe_with_paho.py
```

If you see a traceback with an `SSLError` similar to the following lines, it means that the MQTT server hostname or IP doesn't match the value specified for the `Common Name` attribute when you generated the server certificate file named `server.crt`. Make sure that you check the IP address for the MQTT server (Mosquitto server) and generate the server certificate file and key again with the appropriate IP address or hostname specified for `Common Name`, as explained in `Chapter 3`, *Securing an MQTT 3.1.1 Mosquitto Server*, if you are working with the self-signed certificates we generated. If you are working with self-signed certificates, IP addresses, and a DHCP server, also check that the DHCP server didn't change the IP address for your Mosquitto server:

```
Traceback (most recent call last):
  File "<stdin>", line 1, in <module>
  File "/Users/gaston/HillarMQTT/01/lib/python3.6/site-
packages/paho/mqtt/client.py", line 612, in connect
    return self.reconnect()
  File "/Users/gaston/HillarMQTT/01/lib/python3.6/site-
packages/paho/mqtt/client.py", line 751, in reconnect
    self._tls_match_hostname()
  File "/Users/gaston/HillarMQTT/01/lib/python3.6/site-
packages/paho/mqtt/client.py", line 2331, in _tls_match_hostname
    raise ssl.SSLError('Certificate subject does not match remote
hostname.')
```

Now, follow these steps to use the MQTT.fx GUI utility to publish two messages to the `vehicles/vehiclepi01/tests` topic:

1. Launch MQTT.fx and establish a connection with the MQTT server by following the steps we learned in `Chapter 3`, *Securing an MQTT 3.1.1 Mosquitto Server*.
2. Click **Publish** and enter `vehicles/vehiclepi01/tests` in the drop-down menu at the left-hand side of the **Publish** button.
3. Click **QoS 2** at the right-hand side of the **Publish** button.
4. Enter the following text in the textbox under the **Publish** button: `{"CMD": "UNLOCK_DOORS"}`. Then, click the **Publish** button. MQTT.fx will publish the entered text to the specified topic.
5. Enter the following text in the textbox under the **Publish** button: `{"CMD": "TURN_ON_HEADLIGHTS"}`. Then, click the **Publish** button. MQTT.fx will publish the entered text to the specified topic.

If you don't want to work with the MQTT.fx utility, you can run two `mosquitto_pub` commands to generate MQTT clients that publish messages to the topic. You just need to open another Terminal in macOS or Linux, or another Command Prompt in Windows, go to the directory in which Mosquitto is installed, and run the following commands. In this case, it isn't necessary to specify the –d option. Replace `192.168.1.101` with the IP or hostname for the MQTT server. Remember to replace `ca.crt`, `board001.crt`, and `board001.key` with the full path to these files created in the `board_certificates` directory. The code file for the sample is included in the `mqtt_python_gaston_hillar_04_01` folder, in the `script_01.txt` file:

```
mosquitto_pub -h 192.168.1.101 -V mqttv311 -p 8883 --cafile ca.crt --cert
board001.crt --key board001.key -t vehicles/vehiclepi01/tests -m '{"CMD":
"UNLOCK_DOORS"}' -q 2 --tls-version tlsv1.2

mosquitto_pub -h 192.168.1.101 -V mqttv311 -p 8883 --cafile ca.crt --cert
board001.crt --key board001.key -t vehicles/vehiclepi01/tests -m '{"CMD":
"TURN_ON_HEADLIGHTS"}' -q 2 --tls-version tlsv1.2
```

Go to the device and window in which you executed the Python script. You will see the following output:

```
Result from connect: Connection Accepted.
I've subscribed with QoS: 2
Message received. Topic: vehicles/vehiclepi01/tests. Payload: b'{"CMD":
"UNLOCK_DOORS"}'
Message received. Topic: vehicles/vehiclepi01/tests. Payload: b'{"CMD":
"TURN_ON_HEADLIGHTS"}'
```

The Python program successfully established a secured and encrypted connection with the MQTT server and became a subscriber to the `vehicles/vehiclepi01/tests` topic with a granted QoS level of 2. The program displayed the two messages it has received in the `vehicles/vehiclepi01/tests` topic.

Press *Ctrl* + *C* to stop the execution of the program. The generated MQTT client will close the connection with the MQTT server. You will see an error message similar to the following output because the loop execution is interrupted:

```
Traceback (most recent call last):
  File "subscribe_with_paho.py", line 33, in <module>
    client.loop_forever()
  File "/Users/gaston/HillarMQTT/01/lib/python3.6/site-
packages/paho/mqtt/client.py", line 1481, in loop_forever
    rc = self.loop(timeout, max_packets)
  File "/Users/gaston/HillarMQTT/01/lib/python3.6/site-
packages/paho/mqtt/client.py", line 988, in loop
    socklist = select.select(rlist, wlist, [], timeout)
KeyboardInterrupt
```

Configuring certificates for IoT boards that will work as clients

Now, we will write Python code that will be ready to work on the different IoT boards. Of course, you can work with a single development computer or development board. There is no need to run the code on different devices. We just want to make sure we can write code that will be capable of running on different devices.

Remember to copy the files we created in the previous chapter to a directory on the computer or device that will represent the board that controls a vehicle and that we will use to run a Python script. If you will be working with the same computer or device you have been using so far, you don't need to follow the next step.

We saved the files in a directory called `mqtt_certificates`. Create a `board_certificates` directory on the computer or board you are going to use as the MQTT client for this example. Copy the following three files to this new directory:

- `ca.crt`: Certificate authority certificate file
- `board001.crt`: Client certificate file
- `board001.key`: Client key

Creating a class to represent a vehicle

We will create the following two classes:

- `Vehicle`: This class will represent a vehicle and provide methods that will be called whenever a command has to be processed. In order to keep the example simple, our methods will just print the actions that the vehicle executes after each method is called to the console output. A real-life class that represents a vehicle would interact with the engine, the lights, the actuators, the sensors, and the other different components of the vehicle whenever each method is called.

- `VehicleCommandProcessor`: This class will represent a command processor that will establish a connection with an MQTT server, subscribe to a topic in which the MQTT client will receive messages with commands, analyze the incoming messages, and delegate the execution of the commands to an associated instance of the `Vehicle` class. The `VehicleCommandProcessor` class will declare many static methods that we will specify as the callbacks for the MQTT client.

Create a new Python file named `vehicle_commands.py` in the main virtual environment folder. The following lines declare many variables with the values that identify each of the supported commands for the vehicle. In addition, the code declares many variables with the key string we will use to specify a command and the key we will use to specify a successfully executed command. All these variables are defined with all uppercase because we will use them as constants. The code file for the sample is included in the `mqtt_python_gaston_hillar_04_01` folder, in the `vehicle_commands.py` file:

```
# Key strings
COMMAND_KEY = "CMD"
SUCCESSFULLY_PROCESSED_COMMAND_KEY = "SUCCESSFULLY_PROCESSED_COMMAND"
# Command strings
# Turn on the vehicle's engine.
CMD_TURN_ON_ENGINE = "TURN_ON_ENGINE"
# Turn off the vehicle's engine
CMD_TURN_OFF_ENGINE = "TURN_OFF_ENGINE"
# Close and lock the vehicle's doors
CMD_LOCK_DOORS = "LOCK_DOORS"
# Unlock and open the vehicle's doors
CMD_UNLOCK_DOORS = "UNLOCK_DOORS"
# Park the vehicle
CMD_PARK = "PARK"
# Park the vehicle in a safe place that is configured for the vehicle
CMD_PARK_IN_SAFE_PLACE = "PARK_IN_SAFE_PLACE"
# Turn on the vehicle's headlights
```

```
CMD_TURN_ON_HEADLIGHTS = "TURN_ON_HEADLIGHTS"
# Turn off the vehicle's headlights
CMD_TURN_OFF_HEADLIGHTS = "TURN_OFF_HEADLIGHTS"
# Turn on the vehicle's parking lights, also known as sidelights
CMD_TURN_ON_PARKING_LIGHTS = "TURN_ON_PARKING_LIGHTS"
# Turn off the vehicle's parking lights, also known as sidelights
CMD_TURN_OFF_PARKING_LIGHTS = "TURN_OFF_PARKING_LIGHTS"
# Accelerate the vehicle, that is, press the gas pedal
CMD_ACCELERATE = "ACCELERATE"
# Brake the vehicle, that is, press the brake pedal
CMD_BRAKE = "BRAKE"
# Make the vehicle rotate to the right. We must specify the degrees
# we want the vehicle to rotate right in the value for the DEGREES key
CMD_ROTATE_RIGHT = "ROTATE_RIGHT"
# Make the vehicle rotate to the left. We must specify the degrees
# we want the vehicle to rotate left in the value for the DEGREES key
CMD_ROTATE_LEFT = "ROTATE_LEFT"
# Set the maximum speed that we allow to the vehicle. We must specify
# the desired maximum speed in miles per hour in the value for the MPH key
CMD_SET_MAX_SPEED = "SET_MAX_SPEED"
# Set the minimum speed that we allow to the vehicle. We must specify
# the desired minimum speed in miles per hour in the value for the MPH key
CMD_SET_MIN_SPEED = "SET_MIN_SPEED"
# Degrees key
KEY_DEGREES = "DEGREES"
# Miles per hour key
KEY_MPH = "MPH"
```

The COMMAND_KEY variable defines the key string that defines what the code will understand as the command. Whenever we receive a message that includes the specified key string, we know that the value associated with this key in the dictionary will indicate the command that the message wants the code running in the board to be processed. The MQTT client won't receive messages as dictionaries, and therefore, it is necessary to convert them from strings to dictionaries when they are not just a string.

The SUCCESSFULLY_PROCESSED_COMMAND_KEY variable defines the key string that defines what the code will use as a successfully processed command key in a response message published to the appropriate topic. Whenever we publish a message that includes the specified key string, we know that the value associated with this key in the dictionary will indicate the command that the board has successfully processed.

Create a new Python file, named `vehicle_mqtt_client.py`, in the main virtual environment folder. The following lines declare the necessary imports and the same variables we used in the previous example to establish the connection with the MQTT server. Then, the lines declare the `Vehicle` class. The code file for the sample is included in the `mqtt_python_gaston_hillar_04_01` folder, in the `vehicle_mqtt_client.py` file:

```python
class Vehicle:
    def __init__(self, name):
        self.name = name
        self.min_speed_mph = 0
        self.max_speed_mph = 10

    def print_action_with_name_prefix(self, action):
        print("{}: {}".format(self.name, action))

    def turn_on_engine(self):
        self.print_action_with_name_prefix("Turning on the engine")

    def turn_off_engine(self):
        self.print_action_with_name_prefix("Turning off the engine")

    def lock_doors(self):
        self.print_action_with_name_prefix("Locking doors")

    def unlock_doors(self):
        self.print_action_with_name_prefix("Unlocking doors")

    def park(self):
        self.print_action_with_name_prefix("Parking")

    def park_in_safe_place(self):
        self.print_action_with_name_prefix("Parking in safe place")

    def turn_on_headlights(self):
        self.print_action_with_name_prefix("Turning on headlights")

    def turn_off_headlights(self):
        self.print_action_with_name_prefix("Turning off headlights")

    def turn_on_parking_lights(self):
        self.print_action_with_name_prefix("Turning on parking lights")

    def turn_off_parking_lights(self):
        self.print_action_with_name_prefix("Turning off parking
          lights")

    def accelerate(self):
```

```
        self.print_action_with_name_prefix("Accelerating")

    def brake(self):
        self.print_action_with_name_prefix("Braking")

    def rotate_right(self, degrees):
        self.print_action_with_name_prefix("Rotating right {}
          degrees".format(degrees))

    def rotate_left(self, degrees):
        self.print_action_with_name_prefix("Rotating left {}
          degrees".format(degrees))

    def set_max_speed(self, mph):
        self.max_speed_mph = mph
        self.print_action_with_name_prefix("Setting maximum speed to {}
        MPH".format(mph))

    def set_min_speed(self, mph):
        self.min_speed_mph = mph
        self.print_action_with_name_prefix("Setting minimum speed to {}
        MPH".format(mph))
```

As in the previous example, all the configuration values to establish a connection with the Mosquitto MQTT server are defined in the Python file named `config.py` in the main virtual environment folder. If you want to run this example on a different device, you will have to create a new `config.py` file with the appropriate values and change the line that imports the values from the `config` module to use the new configuration file. Don't forget to replace the `/Users/gaston/board_certificates` value in the `certificates_path` string with the path to the `board_certificates` directory you created. In addition, replace the value for the `mqtt_server_host` with the IP address or hostname for the Mosquitto server or other MQTT server you might decide to use.

We have to specify the vehicle's name in the name required argument. The constructor, that is, the `__init__` method, saves the received name in an attribute with the same name. Then, the constructor sets the initial values for two attributes: `min_speed_mph` and `max_speed_mph`. These attributes establish the minimum and maximum speed values for the vehicle, expressed in miles per hour.

The `Vehicle` class declares the `print_action_with_name_prefix` method that receives a string with the action that is being executed in the `action` argument and prints it with the value saved in the `name` attribute as a prefix. The other methods defined in this class call the `print_action_with_name_prefix` method to print messages indicating the actions that the vehicle is executing, with the vehicle's name as a prefix.

Receiving messages in Python

We will use the recently installed `paho-mqtt` version 1.3.1 module to subscribe to a specific topic and run code when we receive messages in the topic. We will create a `VehicleCommandProcessor` class in the same Python file, named `vehicle_mqtt_client.py`, in the main virtual environment folder. This class will represent a command processor associated to an instance of the previously coded `Vehicle` class, configure the MQTT client and the subscription to the client, and declare the code for the callbacks that are going to be executed when certain events related to MQTT are fired.

We will split the code for the `VehicleCommandProcessor` class into many code snippets to make it easier to understand each code section. You have to add the next lines to the existing `vehicle_mqtt_client.py` Python file. The following lines declare the `VehicleCommandProcessor` class and its constructor, that is, the __init__ method. The code file for the sample is included in the `mqtt_python_gaston_hillar_04_01` folder, in the `vehicle_mqtt_client.py` file:

```
class VehicleCommandProcessor:
    commands_topic = ""
    processed_commands_topic = ""
    active_instance = None

    def __init__(self, name, vehicle):
        self.name = name
        self.vehicle = vehicle
        VehicleCommandProcessor.commands_topic = \
            "vehicles/{}/commands".format(self.name)
        VehicleCommandProcessor.processed_commands_topic = \
            "vehicles/{}/executedcommands".format(self.name)
        self.client = mqtt.Client(protocol=mqtt.MQTTv311)
        VehicleCommandProcessor.active_instance = self
        self.client.on_connect = VehicleCommandProcessor.on_connect
        self.client.on_subscribe = VehicleCommandProcessor.on_subscribe
        self.client.on_message = VehicleCommandProcessor.on_message
        self.client.tls_set(ca_certs = ca_certificate,
            certfile=client_certificate,
            keyfile=client_key)
        self.client.connect(host=mqtt_server_host,
                            port=mqtt_server_port,
                            keepalive=mqtt_keepalive)
```

We have to specify a name for the command processor and the `Vehicle` instance that the command processor will control in the `name` and `vehicle` required arguments. The constructor, that is, the `__init__` method, saves the received `name` and `vehicle` in attributes with the same names. Then, the constructor sets the values for the `commands_topic` and `processed_commands_topic` class attributes. The constructor uses the received `name` to determine the topic name for the commands and for the successfully processed commands, based on the specifications we discussed earlier. The MQTT client will receive messages in the topic name saved in the `command_topic` class attribute, and will publish messages to the topic name saved in the `processed_commands_topic` class attribute.

Then, the constructor creates an instance of the `mqtt.Client` class (`paho.mqtt.client.Client`) that represents an MQTT client and that we will use to communicate with an MQTT server. The code assigns this instance to the `client` attribute (`self.client`). As in our previous example, we want to work with MQTT version 3.11, and therefore, we specified `mqtt.MQTTv311` as the value for the protocol argument.

The code also saves a reference to this instance in the `active_instance` class attribute because we have to access the instance in the static methods that the constructor will specify as callbacks for the different events that the MQTT client fires. We want to have all the methods related to the vehicle command processor in the `VehicleCommandProcessor` class.

Then, the code assigns static methods to attributes of the `self.client` instance. The following table summarizes these assignments:

Attribute	Assigned static method
`client.on_connect`	`VehicleCommandProcessor.on_connect`
`client.on_message`	`VehicleCommandProcessor.on_message`
`client.on_subscribe`	`VehicleCommandProcessor.on_subscribe`

Static methods do not receive either `self` or `cls` as the first argument, and therefore, we can use them as callbacks with the required number of arguments. Note that we will code and analyze these static methods in the next paragraphs.

The call to the `self.client.tls_set` method configures encryption and authentication options. Finally, the constructor calls the `client.connect` method and specifies the values for the `host`, `port`, and `keepalive` arguments. This way, the code asks the MQTT client to establish a connection to the specified MQTT server. Remember that the `connect` method runs with an asynchronous execution, and therefore, it is a non-blocking call.

 If you want to establish a connection with an MQTT server that isn't using TLS, you need to remove the call to the `self.client.tls_set` method. In addition, you need to use the appropriate port instead of the `8883` port that is specified when working with TLS. Remember that the default port when you don't work with TLS is `1883`.

The following lines declare the `on_connect` static method that is part of the `VehicleCommandProcessor` class. You have to add these lines to the existing `vehicle_mqtt_client.py` Python file. The code file for the sample is included in the `mqtt_python_gaston_hillar_04_01` folder, in the `vehicle_mqtt_client.py` file:

```
@staticmethod
def on_connect(client, userdata, flags, rc):
    print("Result from connect: {}".format(
        mqtt.connack_string(rc)))
    # Check whether the result form connect is the CONNACK_ACCEPTED
      connack code
    if rc == mqtt.CONNACK_ACCEPTED:
        # Subscribe to the commands topic filter
        client.subscribe(
            VehicleCommandProcessor.commands_topic,
            qos=2)
```

After a connection has been successfully established with the MQTT server, the specified callback in the `self.client.on_connect` attribute will be executed, that is, the `on_connect` static method (marked with the `@staticmethod` decorator). This static method receives the `mqtt.Client` instance that established the connection with the MQTT server in the client argument.

The code checks the value of the `rc` argument that provides the CONNACK code returned by the MQTT server. If this value matches `mqtt.CONNACK_ACCEPTED`, it means that the MQTT server accepted the connection request, and therefore, the code calls the `client.subscribe` method with `VehicleCommandProcessor.commands_topic` as an argument to subscribe to the topic specified in the `commands_topic` class attribute and specifies a QoS level of 2 for the subscription.

The following lines declare the `on_subscribe` static method that is part of the `VehicleCommandProcessor` class. You have to add these lines to the existing `vehicle_mqtt_client.py` Python file. The code file for the sample is included in the `mqtt_python_gaston_hillar_04_01` folder, in the `vehicle_mqtt_client.py` file:

```python
@staticmethod
def on_subscribe(client, userdata, mid, granted_qos):
    print("I've subscribed with QoS: {}".format(
        granted_qos[0]))
```

The `on_subscribe` static method displays the QoS level granted by the MQTT server for the topic filter we specified. In this case, we just subscribed to a single topic filter, and therefore, the code grabs the first value from the received `granted_qos` array.

The following lines declare the `on_message` static method that is part of the `VehicleCommandProcessor` class. You have to add these lines to the existing `vehicle_mqtt_client.py` Python file. The code file for the sample is included in the `mqtt_python_gaston_hillar_04_01` folder, in the `vehicle_mqtt_client.py` file:

```python
@staticmethod
def on_message(client, userdata, msg):
    if msg.topic == VehicleCommandProcessor.commands_topic:
        print("Received message payload:
        {0}".format(str(msg.payload)))
        try:
            message_dictionary = json.loads(msg.payload)
            if COMMAND_KEY in message_dictionary:
                command = message_dictionary[COMMAND_KEY]
                vehicle =
                VehicleCommandProcessor.active_instance.vehicle
                is_command_executed = False
                if KEY_MPH in message_dictionary:
                    mph = message_dictionary[KEY_MPH]
                else:
                    mph = 0
                if KEY_DEGREES in message_dictionary:
                    degrees = message_dictionary[KEY_DEGREES]
                else:
                    degrees = 0
                command_methods_dictionary = {
                    CMD_TURN_ON_ENGINE: lambda:
                    vehicle.turn_on_engine(),
                    CMD_TURN_OFF_ENGINE: lambda:
                    vehicle.turn_off_engine(),
                    CMD_LOCK_DOORS: lambda: vehicle.lock_doors(),
                    CMD_UNLOCK_DOORS: lambda:
```

```
                          vehicle.unlock_doors(),
                      CMD_PARK: lambda: vehicle.park(),
                      CMD_PARK_IN_SAFE_PLACE: lambda:
                      vehicle.park_in_safe_place(),
                      CMD_TURN_ON_HEADLIGHTS: lambda:
                      vehicle.turn_on_headlights(),
                      CMD_TURN_OFF_HEADLIGHTS: lambda:
                      vehicle.turn_off_headlights(),
                      CMD_TURN_ON_PARKING_LIGHTS: lambda:
                      vehicle.turn_on_parking_lights(),
                      CMD_TURN_OFF_PARKING_LIGHTS: lambda:
                      vehicle.turn_off_parking_lights(),
                      CMD_ACCELERATE: lambda: vehicle.accelerate(),
                      CMD_BRAKE: lambda: vehicle.brake(),
                      CMD_ROTATE_RIGHT: lambda:
                      vehicle.rotate_right(degrees),
                      CMD_ROTATE_LEFT: lambda:
                      vehicle.rotate_left(degrees),
                      CMD_SET_MIN_SPEED: lambda:
                      vehicle.set_min_speed(mph),
                      CMD_SET_MAX_SPEED: lambda:
                      vehicle.set_max_speed(mph),
                  }
              if command in command_methods_dictionary:
                  method = command_methods_dictionary[command]
                  # Call the method
                  method()
                  is_command_executed = True
              if is_command_executed:
          VehicleCommandProcessor.active_instance.
           publish_executed_command_message(message_dictionary)
                  else:
                      print("I've received a message with an
                          unsupported command.")
          except ValueError:
              # msg is not a dictionary
              # No JSON object could be decoded
              print("I've received an invalid message.")
```

Whenever there is a new message received in the topic saved in the `commands_topic` class attribute to which we have subscribed, the specified callback in the `self.client.on_messsage` attribute will be executed, that is, the previously coded `on_message` static method (marked with the `@staticmethod` decorator). This static method receives the `mqtt.Client` instance that established the connection with the MQTT server in the client argument and an `mqtt.MQTTMessage` instance in the `msg` argument.

The `mqtt.MQTTMessage` class describes an incoming message.

The `msg.topic` attribute indicates the topic in which the message has been received. Thus, the static method checks whether the `msg.topic` attribute matches the value in the `commands_topic` class attribute. In this case, whenever the `on_message` method is executed, the value in `msg.topic` will always match the value in the topic class attribute because we just subscribed to one topic. However, if we subscribe to more than one topic, it is always necessary to check which is the topic in which the message was sent and in which we are receiving the message. Hence, we included the code to have a clear idea of how to check the `topic` for the received message.

The code prints the payload for the message that has been received, that is, the `msg.payload` attribute. Then, the code assigns the result of the `json.loads` function to deserialize `msg.payload` to a Python object and assigns the results to the `message_dictionary` local variable. If the contents of `msg.payload` are not JSON, a `ValueError` exception will be captured, the code will print a message indicating that the message doesn't include a valid command, and no more code will be executed in the static method. If the contents of `msg.payload` are JSON, we will have a dictionary in the `message_dictionary` local variable.

Then, the code checks whether the value saved in the COMMAND_KEY string is included in the `message_dictionary` dictionary. If the expression evaluates to `True`, it means that the JSON message converted to a dictionary includes a command that we have to process. However, before we can process the command, we have to check which is the command, and therefore, it is necessary to retrieve the value associated with the key equivalent to the value saved in the COMMAND_KEY string. The code is capable of running specific code when the value is any of the commands that we have analyzed as requirements.

The code uses the `active_instance` class attribute that has a reference to the active `VehicleCommandProcessor` instance to call the necessary methods for the associated vehicle based on the command that has to be processed. We had to declare the callbacks as static methods, and therefore, we use this class attribute to access the active instance. Once the command has been successfully processed, the code sets the `is_command_executed` flag to `True`. Finally, the code checks the value of this flag, and if it is equal to `True`, the code calls the `publish_executed_command_message` for the `VehicleCommandProcessor` instance saved in the `active_instance` class attribute.

Of course, in a real-life example, we should add more validations. The previous code is simplified to allow us to keep our focus on MQTT.

The following lines declare the `publish_executed_command_message` method that is part of the `VehicleCommandProcessor` class. You have to add these lines to the existing `vehicle_mqtt_client.py` Python file. The code file for the sample is included in the `mqtt_python_gaston_hillar_04_01` folder, in the `vehicle_mqtt_client.py` file:

```
def publish_executed_command_message(self, message):
    response_message = json.dumps({
        SUCCESFULLY_PROCESSED_COMMAND_KEY:
            message[COMMAND_KEY]})
    result = self.client.publish(
        topic=self.__class__.processed_commands_topic,
        payload=response_message)
    return result
```

The `publish_executed_command_message` method receives the message dictionary that has been received with the command in the message argument. The method calls the `json.dumps` function to serialize a dictionary to a JSON-formatted string with the response message that indicates the command has been successfully processed. Finally, the code calls the `client.publish` method with the `processed_commands_topic` variable as the topic argument and the JSON-formatted string (`response_message`) in the `payload` argument.

In this case, we are not evaluating the response received from the `publish` method. In addition, we are using the default value for the `qos` argument that specifies the desired quality of service. Thus, we will publish this message with a QoS level equal to 0. In Chapter 5, *Testing and Improving our Vehicle Control Solution in Python*, we will work with more advanced scenarios in which we will add code to check the results of the method and we will add code to the `on_publish` callback that is fired when a message is successfully published, as we did in our previous example. In this case, we use QoS level 2 only for the messages that we receive with the commands.

Working with multiple calls to the loop method

The following lines declare the `process_incoming_commands` method that is part of the `VehicleCommandProcessor` class. You have to add these lines to the existing `vehicle_mqtt_client.py` Python file. The code file for the sample is included in the `mqtt_python_gaston_hillar_04_01` folder, in the `vehicle_mqtt_client.py` file:

```
def process_incoming_commands(self):
    self.client.loop()
```

The `process_incoming_commands` method calls the `loop` method for the MQTT client and ensures communication with the MQTT server is carried out. Think about the call to the `loop` method as synchronizing your mailbox. Any pending messages to be published in the outgoing box will be sent, any incoming messages will arrive to the inbox, and the events that we have previously analyzed will be fired. This way, the vehicle command processor will receive messages and process commands.

Finally, the following lines declare the main block of code. You have to add these lines to the existing `vehicle_mqtt_client.py` Python file. The code file for the sample is included in the `mqtt_python_gaston_hillar_04_01` folder, in the `vehicle_mqtt_client.py` file:

```
if __name__ == "__main__":
    vehicle = Vehicle("vehiclepi01")
    vehicle_command_processor = VehicleCommandProcessor("vehiclepi01",
        vehicle)
    while True:
        # Process messages and the commands every 1 second
        vehicle_command_processor.process_incoming_commands()
        time.sleep(1)
```

The __main__ method creates an instance of the `Vehicle` class, named vehicle, with `"vehiclepi01"` as the value for the name argument. The next line creates an instance of the `VehicleCommandProcessor` class, named `vehicle_command_processor`, with `"vehiclepi01"` and the previously created `Vehicle` instance, *X*, as the values for the name and `vehicle` arguments. This way, `vehicle_command_processor` will delegate the execution of the commands to instance methods in `vehicle`.

The constructor for the `VehicleCommandProcessor` class will subscribe to the `vehicles/vehiclepi01/commands` topic in the MQTT server, and therefore, we must publish messages to this topic in order to send the commands that the code will process. Whenever a command is successfully processed, new messages will be published to the `vehicles/vehiclepi01/executedcommands` topic. Hence, we must subscribe to this topic to check the commands that the vehicle has executed.

The while loop calls the `vehicle_command_processor.process_commands` method and sleeps for one second. The `process_commands` method calls the loop method for the MQTT client and ensures communication with the MQTT server is carried out.

 There is also a threaded interface that we can run by calling the `loop_start` method for the MQTT client. This way, we can avoid multiple calls to the loop method. However, we call the loop method to make it easier to debug the code and understand how everything works under the hood. We will work with the threaded interfaces in Chapter 5, *Testing and Improving our Vehicle Control Solution in Python*.

Test your knowledge

Let's see whether you can answer the following questions correctly:

1. Which of the following Python modules is the Paho Python Client?
    1. `paho-mqtt`
    2. `paho-client-pip`
    3. `paho-python-client`

2. To establish a connection with an MQTT server that uses TLS, which method do you have to call for the `paho.mqtt.client.Client` instance before calling connect?
    1. `connect_with_tls`
    2. `tls_set`
    3. `configure_tls`

3. After the `paho.mqtt.client.Client` instance establishes a connection with the MQTT server, the callback assigned to which of the following attributes will be called?
    1. `on_connection`
    2. `on_connect`
    3. `connect_callback`

4. After the `paho.mqtt.client.Client` instance receives a message from one of the topic filters to which it has subscribed, the callback assigned to which of the following attributes will be called?
    1. `on_message_arrived`
    2. `on_message`
    3. `message_arrived_callback`

5. Which of the following methods of a `paho.mqtt.client.Client` instance calls the loop method for us in an infinite blocking loop?
    1. `infinite_loop`
    2. `loop_while_true`
    3. `loop_forever`

The right answers are included in the `Appendix`, *Solutions*.

Summary

In this chapter, we analyzed the requirements to control a vehicle with MQTT messages. We defined the topics that we would use and the commands that would be part of the messages' payloads to control a vehicle. Then, we worked with the Paho Python Client to write Python code that connected an MQTT client to the MQTT server.

We understood the methods we needed to call for the Paho Python Client and their parameters. We analyzed how callbacks worked and we wrote code to subscribe to topic filters as well as to receive and process messages.

We wrote code that processed commands for a vehicle with Python. The code is able to run on different IoT platforms, including Raspberry Pi 3 family boards, Qualcomm DragonBoard, BeagleBone Black, MinnowBoard Turbot, LattePanda, UP squared, and also on any computer that is capable of executing Python 3.6.x code. We worked with the network loop for the MQTT client in Python.

Now that we have understood the basics to use Python to work with MQTT, we will use and improve our vehicle control solution with MQTT messages and Python code and we will take advantage of additional MQTT features, which are the topics we are going to discuss in Chapter 5, *Testing and Improving our Vehicle Control Solution in Python*.

5
Testing and Improving Our Vehicle Control Solution in Python

In this chapter, we will use our vehicle control solution with MQTT messages and Python code. We will learn how to process commands received in MQTT messages with Python code. We will write Python code to compose and send MQTT messages with commands. We will work with the blocking and threaded network loops and we will understand their difference. Finally, we will take advantage of the last will and testament feature. We will take an in-depth look at the following:

- Processing commands with Python
- Sending messages with Python
- Working with the network loop with Python
- Working with last will and testament with Python
- Working with retained last will messages
- Understanding blocking and non-blocking code
- Using the threaded client interface

Processing commands with Python

In Chapter 4, *Writing Code to Control a Vehicle with Python and MQTT Messages*, we coded a solution that was capable of processing commands for a vehicle received as MQTT messages with Python code. Now, we want to make a vehicle process many commands to check how all the pieces work together. We want to execute the following commands:

```
{"CMD": "LOCK_DOORS"}
{"CMD": "TURN_OFF_PARKING_LIGHTS"}
```

```
{"CMD": "SET_MAX_SPEED", "MPH": 10}
{"CMD": "SET_MIN_SPEED", "MPH": 1}
{"CMD": "TURN_ON_ENGINE"}
{"CMD": "TURN_ON_HEADLIGHTS"}
{"CMD": "ACCELERATE"}
{"CMD": "ROTATE_RIGHT", "DEGREES": 45}
{"CMD": "ACCELERATE"}
{"CMD": "TURN_ON_PARKING_LIGHTS"}
{"CMD": "BRAKE"}
{"CMD": "TURN_OFF_ENGINE"}
```

Make sure the Mosquitto server, or any other MQTT server you might want to use for this example, is running.

Launch MQTT.fx and follow all the steps explained in Chapter 4, *Writing Code to Control a Vehicle with Python and MQTT Messages*, to configure a connection with TLS and TLS authentication, if you didn't establish a previous secure connection to the MQTT server with MQTT.fx. Then, click on the **Connect** button.

Click **Subscribe** and enter vehicles/vehiclepi01/executedcommands in the drop-down menu on the left-hand side of the **Subscribe** button. Then, click the **Subscribe** button. MQTT.fx will display a new panel on the left-hand side with the topic filter to which we have subscribed with QoS level 0.

Then, execute the following line to start the vehicle controller example in any computer or device that you want to use as the MQTT client that uses Linux or macOS:

```
python3 subscribe_with_paho.py
```

In Windows, you must execute the following line:

```
python subscribe_with_paho.py
```

Keep the code running on your local computer or on the IoT board you have chosen to use as the vehicle controller for this example.

In MQTT.fx, click **Publish** and enter vehicles/vehiclepi01/commands in the drop-down menu on the left-hand side of the **Publish** button. Click **QoS 2** because we want to use QoS level 2.

Enter the following text in the textbox below the **Publish** button: {"CMD": "LOCK_DOORS"}

Then, click the **Publish** button. MQTT.fx will publish the entered text to the specified topic with QoS level 2.

Go to the window in which you can see the output generated by the Python code that receives the messages and controls the vehicle. If you are running the code on an IoT board, you might be using an SSH terminal or a screen connected to the IoT board. If you are running the code on your local computer, go to Terminal or Command Prompt, based on the operating system you are using. You will see the following output:

```
Result from connect: Connection Accepted.
Received message payload: b'{"CMD": "LOCK_DOORS"}'
vehiclepi01: Locking doors
```

The code has received the message with the command, the `Vehicle` instance executed the `lock_doors` method, and the output displays the results of executing this code.

Go back to MQTT.fx, click **Subscribe** and you will see a new message has arrived in the `vehicles/vehiclepi01/executedcommands` topic with the following payload: `{"SUCCESSFULLY_PROCESSED_COMMAND": "LOCK_DOORS"}`. The following screenshot shows the received message in MQTT.fx:

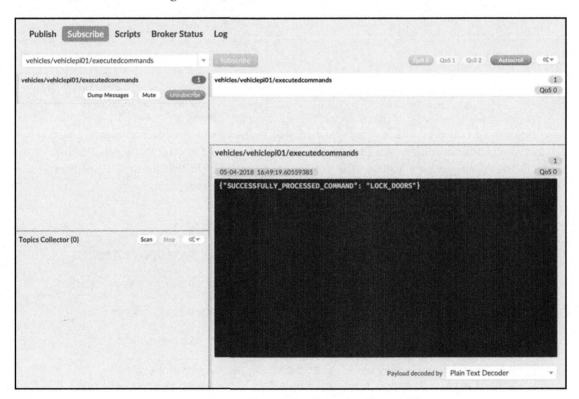

Now, repeat the following procedure for each of the commands included in the previously shown list. We want our vehicle control application to process each of those commands received in MQTT messages with QoS level 2. Remove the existing text and enter the text for the JSON string in the textbox under the **Publish** button and then click the **Publish** button. MQTT.fx will publish the entered text to the specified topic with QoS level 2:

```
{"CMD": "TURN_OFF_PARKING_LIGHTS"}

{"CMD": "SET_MAX_SPEED", "MPH": 10}

{"CMD": "SET_MIN_SPEED", "MPH": 1}

{"CMD": "TURN_ON_ENGINE"}

{"CMD": "TURN_ON_HEADLIGHTS"}

{"CMD": "ACCELERATE"}

{"CMD": "ROTATE_RIGHT", "DEGREES": 45}

{"CMD": "ACCELERATE"}

{"CMD": "TURN_ON_PARKING_LIGHTS"}

{"CMD": "BRAKE"}

{"CMD": "TURN_OFF_ENGINE"}
```

Go to the window in which you can see the output generated by the Python code that receives the messages and controls the vehicle. You will see the following output that indicates that all the commands have been received and processed:

```
Result from connect: Connection Accepted.
Received message payload: b'{"CMD": "LOCK_DOORS"}'
vehiclepi01: Locking doors
Received message payload: b'{"CMD": "TURN_OFF_PARKING_LIGHTS"}'
vehiclepi01: Turning off parking lights
Received message payload: b'{"CMD": "SET_MAX_SPEED", "MPH": 10}'
vehiclepi01: Setting maximum speed to 10 MPH
Received message payload: b'{"CMD": "SET_MIN_SPEED", "MPH": 1}'
vehiclepi01: Setting minimum speed to 1 MPH
Received message payload: b'{"CMD": "TURN_ON_ENGINE"}'
vehiclepi01: Turning on the engine
Received message payload: b'{"CMD": "TURN_ON_HEADLIGHTS"}'
vehiclepi01: Turning on headlights
Received message payload: b'{"CMD": "ACCELERATE"}'
vehiclepi01: Accelerating
```

```
Received message payload: b'{"CMD": "ROTATE_RIGHT", "DEGREES": 45}'
vehiclepi01: Rotating right 45 degrees
Received message payload: b'{"CMD": "ACCELERATE"}'
vehiclepi01: Accelerating
Received message payload: b'{"CMD": "TURN_ON_PARKING_LIGHTS"}'
vehiclepi01: Turning on parking lights
Received message payload: b'{"CMD": "BRAKE"}'
vehiclepi01: Braking
Received message payload: b'{"CMD": "TURN_OFF_ENGINE"}'
vehiclepi01: Turning off the engine
```

Go back to MQTT.fx, click **Subscribe,** and you will see a total of 12 messages that have arrived in the vehicles/vehiclepi01/executedcommands topic. You can easily check the contents of the payload for each of the received messages by clicking on the panel that represents each of them on the right-hand side of the window. The following screenshot shows the last received message in MQTT.fx:

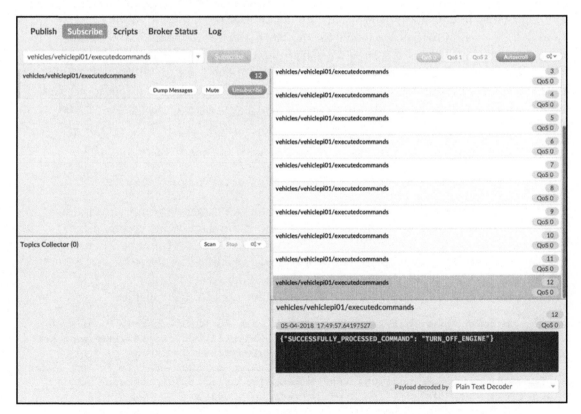

Now, we will use the Mosquitto command-line utilities to subscribe to the vehicles/vehiclepi01/executedcommands topic and publish many MQTT messages with the JSON strings with the commands to the vehicles/vehiclepi01/commands topic. This time, we will publish the following commands:

```
{"CMD": "UNLOCK_DOORS"}
{"CMD": "LOCK_DOORS"}
{"CMD": "SET_MAX_SPEED", "MPH": 20}
{"CMD": "SET_MIN_SPEED", "MPH": 5}
{"CMD": "TURN_ON_ENGINE"}
{"CMD": "ACCELERATE"}
{"CMD": "ROTATE_LEFT", "DEGREES": 15}
{"CMD": "ROTATE_LEFT", "DEGREES": 20}
{"CMD": "BRAKE"}
{"CMD": "TURN_OFF_ENGINE"}
```

Open another Terminal in macOS or Linux, or another Command Prompt in Windows, go to the directory in which Mosquitto is installed, and run the following command. Replace 192.168.1.1 with the IP or hostname for the MQTT server. Remember to replace ca.crt, board001.crt, and board001.key with the full path to these files, created in the board_certificates directory. Leave the window opened and the utility will display all the messages received in the vehicles/vehiclepi01/executedcommands topic. The code file for the sample is included in the mqtt_python_gaston_hillar_05_01 folder, in the script_01.txt file:

```
mosquitto_sub -h 192.168.1.1 -V mqttv311 -p 8883 --cafile ca.crt --
cert device001.crt --key device001.key -t
vehicles/vehiclepi01/executedcommands --tls-version tlsv1.2
```

Open another Terminal in macOS or Linux, or another Command Prompt in Windows, go to the directory in which Mosquitto is installed, and run the following commands to publish messages with commands to the vehicles/vehiclepi01/commands topic with QoS level 2. Make the same replacements previously explained for the mosquitto_sub command. The code file for the sample is included in the mqtt_python_gaston_hillar_05_01 folder, in the script_02.txt file:

```
mosquitto_pub -h 192.168.1.1 -V mqttv311 -p 8883 --cafile ca.crt --
cert board001.crt --key board001.key -t vehicles/vehiclepi01/commands -m
'{"CMD": "UNLOCK_DOORS"}' -q 2 --tls-version tlsv1.2
    mosquitto_pub -h 192.168.1.1 -V mqttv311 -p 8883 --cafile ca.crt --cert
board001.crt --key board001.key -t vehicles/vehiclepi01/commands -m
'{"CMD": "LOCK_DOORS"}' -q 2 --tls-version tlsv1.2
    mosquitto_pub -h 192.168.1.1 -V mqttv311 -p 8883 --cafile ca.crt --cert
board001.crt --key board001.key -t vehicles/vehiclepi01/commands -m
'{"CMD": "SET_MAX_SPEED", "MPH": 20}' -q 2 --tls-version tlsv1.2
```

```
    mosquitto_pub -h 192.168.1.1 -V mqttv311 -p 8883 --cafile ca.crt --cert
board001.crt --key board001.key -t vehicles/vehiclepi01/commands -m
'{"CMD": "SET_MIN_SPEED", "MPH": 5}' -q 2 --tls-version tlsv1.2
    mosquitto_pub -h 192.168.1.1 -V mqttv311 -p 8883 --cafile ca.crt --cert
board001.crt --key board001.key -t vehicles/vehiclepi01/commands -m
'{"CMD": "TURN_ON_ENGINE"}' -q 2 --tls-version tlsv1.2
    mosquitto_pub -h 192.168.1.1 -V mqttv311 -p 8883 --cafile ca.crt --cert
board001.crt --key board001.key -t vehicles/vehiclepi01/commands -m
'{"CMD": "ACCELERATE"}' -q 2 --tls-version tlsv1.2
    mosquitto_pub -h 192.168.1.1 -V mqttv311 -p 8883 --cafile ca.crt --cert
board001.crt --key board001.key -t vehicles/vehiclepi01/commands -m
'{"CMD": "ROTATE_LEFT", "DEGREES": 15}' -q 2 --tls-version tlsv1.2
    mosquitto_pub -h 192.168.1.1 -V mqttv311 -p 8883 --cafile ca.crt --cert
board001.crt --key board001.key -t vehicles/vehiclepi01/commands -m
'{"CMD": "ROTATE_LEFT", "DEGREES": 20}' -q 2 --tls-version tlsv1.2
    mosquitto_pub -h 192.168.1.1 -V mqttv311 -p 8883 --cafile ca.crt --cert
board001.crt --key board001.key -t vehicles/vehiclepi01/commands -m
'{"CMD": "BRAKE"}' -q 2 --tls-version tlsv1.2
    mosquitto_pub -h 192.168.1.1 -V mqttv311 -p 8883 --cafile ca.crt --cert
board001.crt --key board001.key -t vehicles/vehiclepi01/commands -m
'{"CMD": "TURN_OFF_ENGINE"}' -q 2 --tls-version tlsv1.2
```

After you run the previous commands, the `VehicleCommandProcessor` class will receive these commands and process them. After a few seconds, you will see the following output in the window that is executing the `mosquitto_sub` utility:

```
{"SUCCESSFULLY_PROCESSED_COMMAND": "UNLOCK_DOORS"}
{"SUCCESSFULLY_PROCESSED_COMMAND": "LOCK_DOORS"}
{"SUCCESSFULLY_PROCESSED_COMMAND": "SET_MAX_SPEED"}
{"SUCCESSFULLY_PROCESSED_COMMAND": "SET_MIN_SPEED"}
{"SUCCESSFULLY_PROCESSED_COMMAND": "TURN_ON_ENGINE"}
{"SUCCESSFULLY_PROCESSED_COMMAND": "ACCELERATE"}
{"SUCCESSFULLY_PROCESSED_COMMAND": "ROTATE_LEFT"}
{"SUCCESSFULLY_PROCESSED_COMMAND": "ROTATE_LEFT"}
{"SUCCESSFULLY_PROCESSED_COMMAND": "BRAKE"}
{"SUCCESSFULLY_PROCESSED_COMMAND": "TURN_OFF_ENGINE"}
```

 Note that the MQTT.fx utility will also receive the messages because it stayed subscribed to the `vehicles/vehiclepi01/executedcommands` topic.

Go to the window in which you can see the output generated by the Python code that receives the messages and controls the vehicle. You will see the following output, which indicates that all the commands have been received and processed:

```
Result from connect: Connection Accepted.
Received message payload: b'{"CMD": "UNLOCK_DOORS"}'
vehiclepi01: Unlocking doors
Received message payload: b'{"CMD": "LOCK_DOORS"}'
vehiclepi01: Locking doors
Received message payload: b'{"CMD": "SET_MAX_SPEED", "MPH": 20}'
vehiclepi01: Setting maximum speed to 20 MPH
Received message payload: b'{"CMD": "SET_MIN_SPEED", "MPH": 5}'
vehiclepi01: Setting minimum speed to 5 MPH
Received message payload: b'{"CMD": "TURN_ON_ENGINE"}'
vehiclepi01: Turning on the engine
Received message payload: b'{"CMD": "ACCELERATE"}'
vehiclepi01: Accelerating
Received message payload: b'{"CMD": "ROTATE_LEFT", "DEGREES": 15}'
vehiclepi01: Rotating left 15 degrees
Received message payload: b'{"CMD": "ROTATE_LEFT", "DEGREES": 20}'
vehiclepi01: Rotating left 20 degrees
Received message payload: b'{"CMD": "BRAKE"}'
vehiclepi01: Braking
Received message payload: b'{"CMD": "TURN_OFF_ENGINE"}'
vehiclepi01: Turning off the engine
```

Sending messages with Python

So far, we have been publishing MQTT messages to control the vehicle with GUI and command-line tools. Now, we will write code in Python to publish the commands to control each vehicle and check the results of the execution of these commands. Of course, GUI utilities, such as MQTT.fx and the Mosquitto command-line utilities, are extremely useful. However, after we know that things are working as we expect, we can write the necessary code to perform tests in the same programming language we are using to run the code on the IoT board.

Now, we are going to code a Python client that will publish messages to the vehicles/vehiclepi01/commands topic and will subscribe to the vehicles/vehiclepi01/executedcommands topic. We will code both a publisher and a subscriber. This way, we will be able to design applications that can talk to IoT devices with MQTT messages, with Python as the programming language for the client applications. Specifically, the applications will be able to communicate through an MQTT server with Python code in all the publisher and subscriber devices.

We can run the Python client on any other computer or IoT board that is capable of executing Python 3.x.

In Chapter 4, *Writing Code to Control a Vehicle with Python and MQTT Messages*, we created a Python file named config.py in the main virtual environment folder. In this file, we defined many configuration values that were used to establish a connection with the Mosquitto MQTT server. This way, all the configuration values were included in a specific Python script. If you need to make changes to this file to configure the application that will compose and send commands in MQTT messages to control the vehicle, make sure you review the explanations included in Chapter 4, *Writing Code to Control a Vehicle with Python and MQTT Messages*.

Now, we will create a new Python file named vehicle_mqtt_remote_control.py in the main virtual environment folder. We will create many functions that we will assign as the callbacks to the events in the MQTT client. In addition, we will declare variables, a helper class, and a helper function to make it easy to publish a message with a command and the required values for the command. The following lines show the code that defines the variables, the helper class, and the functions. The code file for the sample is included in the mqtt_python_gaston_hillar_05_01 folder, in the vehicle_mqtt_remote_control.py file:

```python
from config import *
from vehicle_commands import *
import paho.mqtt.client as mqtt
import time
import json


vehicle_name = "vehiclepi01"
commands_topic = "vehicles/{}/commands".format(vehicle_name)
processed_commands_topic =
"vehicles/{}/executedcommands".format(vehicle_name)


class LoopControl:
    is_last_command_processed = False


def on_connect(client, userdata, flags, rc):
    print("Result from connect: {}".format(
        mqtt.connack_string(rc)))
    # Check whether the result form connect is the CONNACK_ACCEPTED
```

```
            connack code
    if rc == mqtt.CONNACK_ACCEPTED:
        # Subscribe to the commands topic filter
        client.subscribe(
            processed_commands_topic,
            qos=2)


def on_message(client, userdata, msg):
    if msg.topic == processed_commands_topic:
        print(str(msg.payload))
        if str(msg.payload).count(CMD_TURN_OFF_ENGINE) > 0:
            LoopControl.is_last_command_processed = True


def on_subscribe(client, userdata, mid, granted_qos):
    print("Subscribed with QoS: {}".format(granted_qos[0]))

def build_command_message(command_name, key="", value=""):
    if key:
        # The command requires a key
        command_message = json.dumps({
            COMMAND_KEY: command_name,
            key: value})
    else:
        # The command doesn't require a key
        command_message = json.dumps({
            COMMAND_KEY: command_name})
    return command_message

def publish_command(client, command_name, key="", value=""):
    command_message = build_command_message(
        command_name, key, value)
    result = client.publish(topic=commands_topic, payload=command_message,
qos=2)
client.loop()
time.sleep(1)
return result
```

The first line imports the variables we have declared in our well-known `config.py` file. The code declares the `vehicle_name` variable that saves a string with "`vehiclepi01`" and that we can easily replace with the name of the vehicle that we want to control. Our main goal is to build and publish command messages to the topic specified in the `commands_topic` variable. We will subscribe to the topic specified in the `processed_commands_topic` variable.

The `LoopControl` class declares a class attribute named `is_last_command_processed` initialized to `False`. We will use this class attribute as a flag to control the network loop.

The `on_connect` function is the callback that will be executed once a successful connection has been established with the MQTT server. The code checks the value of the `rc` argument that provides the CONNACK code returned by the MQTT server. If this value matches `mqtt.CONNACK_ACCEPTED`, it means that the MQTT server accepted the connection request, and therefore, the code calls the `client.subscribe` method for the MQTT client received in the `client` argument to subscribe to the topic name saved in the `processed_commands_topic` with a QoS level of 0.

The `on_message` function will be executed each time a new message arrives to the topic to which we have subscribed. The function just prints the raw string with the payload of the received message. If the payload includes the string saved in the `CMD_TURN_OFF_ENGINE` constant, we assume the last command was successfully executed and the code sets the `LoopControl.is_last_command_processed` to `True`. This way, we will control the network loop based on the feedback provided by the vehicle with MQTT messages that indicate the processed commands.

The `on_subscribe` function will be called when the subscription has been successfully completed.

The next table summarizes the functions that will be called based on the received responses from the MQTT server:

Response from the MQTT server	Function that will be called
CONNACK	on_connnect
SUBACK	on_subscribe
PUBLISH	on_message

The `build_command_message` function receives the command name, the key, and the value that provide the necessary information to build the string with the JSON key-value pairs that compose a command in the `command_name`, `key`, and `value` arguments. Note that the last two arguments are optional and their default value is an empty string. The function creates a dictionary and saves the results of serializing the dictionary to a JSON-formatted string in the `command_message` local variable. The `COMMAND_KEY` constant is the first key for the dictionary and the `command_name` received as an argument, the value that composes the first key-value pair. Finally, the function returns the `command_message` string.

The `publish_command` function receives the MQTT client, the command name, the key, and the value that provide the necessary information to execute the command in the `client`, `command_name`, `key`, and `value` arguments. As in the `build_command_message` function, the key and value arguments are optional and their default value is an empty string. The function calls the previously explained `build_command_message` function with the `command_name`, `key`, and `value` arguments it received and saves the result in the `command_message` local variable. Then, the code calls the `client.publish` method to publish the `command_message` JSON-formatted string to the topic name saved in the `commands_topic` variable with a QoS level of 2.

The next line calls the `client.loop` method to ensure communication with the MQTT server is carried out and sleeps for one second. This way, the message will be published and the application will wait one second.

Working with the network loop with Python

Now, we will use the previously coded `functions` in a __main__ method that will publish many commands included in the MQTT messages that the code that controls the vehicle will process. You have to add the next lines to the existing `vehicle_mqtt_remote_control.py` Python file. The following lines show the code for the __main__ method, that is, the main block of code. The code file for the sample is included in the `mqtt_python_gaston_hillar_05_01` folder, in the `vehicle_mqtt_remote_control.py` file:

```python
if __name__ == "__main__":
    client = mqtt.Client(protocol=mqtt.MQTTv311)
    client.on_connect = on_connect
    client.on_subscribe = on_subscribe
    client.on_message = on_message
    client.tls_set(ca_certs = ca_certificate,
        certfile=client_certificate,
        keyfile=client_key)
    client.connect(host=mqtt_server_host,
        port=mqtt_server_port,
        keepalive=mqtt_keepalive)
    publish_command(client, CMD_SET_MAX_SPEED, KEY_MPH, 30)
    publish_command(client, CMD_SET_MIN_SPEED, KEY_MPH, 8)
    publish_command(client, CMD_LOCK_DOORS)
    publish_command(client, CMD_TURN_ON_ENGINE)
    publish_command(client, CMD_ROTATE_RIGHT, KEY_DEGREES, 15)
    publish_command(client, CMD_ACCELERATE)
    publish_command(client, CMD_ROTATE_RIGHT, KEY_DEGREES, 25)
```

```
publish_command(client, CMD_ACCELERATE)
publish_command(client, CMD_ROTATE_LEFT, KEY_DEGREES, 15)
publish_command(client, CMD_ACCELERATE)
publish_command(client, CMD_TURN_OFF_ENGINE)
while LoopControl.is_last_command_processed == False:
    # Process messages and the commands every 500 milliseconds
    client.loop()
    time.sleep(0.5)
client.disconnect()
client.loop()
```

The first lines of code are similar to the first Python example we coded. After calling the client.connect method, the code calls the publish_command command many times to build and publish the messages with the commands.

The while loop calls the client.loop method to ensure communication with the MQTT server is carried out and sleeps for 500 milliseconds, that is, 0.5 seconds. After the last command is processed, the LoopControl.is_last_command_processed class variable is set to True and the while loop ends its execution. When this happens, the code calls the client.disconnect method and finally the client.loop method to make sure that the disconnect request is processed.

If we don't call the client.loop method after calling client.disconnect, the program can finish its execution without sending the request to disconnect to the MQTT server. In the next sections, we will work with the last will and testament feature and we will note that the ways in which a client is disconnected have an important impact on the usage of this feature.

In this case, we don't want the loop to run forever because we have a specific goal of composing and sending a set of commands. Once we are sure that the last command has been processed, we close the connection with the MQTT server.

Make sure that the code that controls vehiclepi01 is running, that is, the vehicle_mqtt_client.py Python script that we coded in Chapter 4, *Writing Code to Control a Vehicle with Python and MQTT Messages*, is running.

Then, execute the following line to start the vehicle remote control example on any computer or device that you want to use as the MQTT client and uses Linux or macOS:

```
python3 vehicle_mqtt_remote_control.py
```

In Windows, you must execute the following line:

```
python vehicle_mqtt_remote_control.py
```

Keep the code running on your local computer or on the IoT board you have chosen to use as the vehicle remote control for this example.

Go to the device and window in which you executed the previous Python script, named `vehicle_mqtt_remote_control.py`. You will see the following output. The Python code will show all the messages received in the `vehicles/vehiclepi01/executedcommands` topic. The program will end its execution after the vehicle indicates that it has successfully processed the `TURN_OFF_ENGINE` command:

```
Result from connect: Connection Accepted.
Subscribed with QoS: 2
b'{"SUCCESSFULLY_PROCESSED_COMMAND": "SET_MAX_SPEED"}'
b'{"SUCCESSFULLY_PROCESSED_COMMAND": "SET_MIN_SPEED"}'
b'{"SUCCESSFULLY_PROCESSED_COMMAND": "LOCK_DOORS"}'
b'{"SUCCESSFULLY_PROCESSED_COMMAND": "TURN_ON_ENGINE"}'
b'{"SUCCESSFULLY_PROCESSED_COMMAND": "ROTATE_RIGHT"}'
b'{"SUCCESSFULLY_PROCESSED_COMMAND": "ACCELERATE"}'
b'{"SUCCESSFULLY_PROCESSED_COMMAND": "ROTATE_RIGHT"}'
b'{"SUCCESSFULLY_PROCESSED_COMMAND": "ACCELERATE"}'
b'{"SUCCESSFULLY_PROCESSED_COMMAND": "ROTATE_LEFT"}'
b'{"SUCCESSFULLY_PROCESSED_COMMAND": "ACCELERATE"}'
b'{"SUCCESSFULLY_PROCESSED_COMMAND": "TURN_OFF_ENGINE"}'
```

Go to the device and window in which you executed the Python script that controlled the vehicle and processed the received commands, that is, `vehicle_mqtt_client.py`. You will see the following output:

```
Received message payload: b'{"CMD": "SET_MAX_SPEED", "MPH": 30}'
vehiclepi01: Setting maximum speed to 30 MPH
Received message payload: b'{"CMD": "SET_MIN_SPEED", "MPH": 8}'
vehiclepi01: Setting minimum speed to 8 MPH
Received message payload: b'{"CMD": "LOCK_DOORS"}'
vehiclepi01: Locking doors
Received message payload: b'{"CMD": "TURN_ON_ENGINE"}'
vehiclepi01: Turning on the engine
Received message payload: b'{"CMD": "ROTATE_RIGHT", "DEGREES": 15}'
vehiclepi01: Rotating right 15 degrees
Received message payload: b'{"CMD": "ACCELERATE"}'
vehiclepi01: Accelerating
Received message payload: b'{"CMD": "ROTATE_RIGHT", "DEGREES": 25}'
vehiclepi01: Rotating right 25 degrees
Received message payload: b'{"CMD": "ACCELERATE"}'
```

```
vehiclepi01: Accelerating
Received message payload: b'{"CMD": "ROTATE_LEFT", "DEGREES": 15}'
vehiclepi01: Rotating left 15 degrees
Received message payload: b'{"CMD": "ACCELERATE"}'
vehiclepi01: Accelerating
Received message payload: b'{"CMD": "TURN_OFF_ENGINE"}'
vehiclepi01: Turning off the engine
```

The following screenshot shows two Terminal windows running on a computer with macOS. The Terminal on the left-hand side is displaying the messages shown by the Python client that publishes commands and works as the remote control for the vehicle, that is, the `vehicle_mqtt_remote_control.py` script. The Terminal on the right-hand side is displaying the results of running the code for the Python client that controls the vehicle and processes the received commands, that is, the `vehicle_mqtt_client.py` script:

Working with last will and testament with Python

Now, we will check what happens if the MQTT client that represents our vehicle remote control application disconnects unexpectedly from the MQTT server with the code we have written so far. Pay attention to all the steps because we will manually interrupt the execution of the vehicle remote control program to understand a specific problem that we will solve by taking advantage of the last will and testament feature.

Execute the following line to start the vehicle remote control example on any computer or device that you want to use as the MQTT client and uses Linux or macOS:

```
python3 vehicle_mqtt_remote_control.py
```

In Windows, you must execute the following line:

```
python vehicle_mqtt_remote_control.py
```

Go to the device and window on which you executed the previous Python script, named `vehicle_mqtt_remote_control.py`. After you see the following output, press *Ctrl + C* to interrupt the execution of the script before all the commands are processed:

```
Result from connect: Connection Accepted.
Subscribed with QoS: 2
b'{"SUCCESSFULLY_PROCESSED_COMMAND": "SET_MAX_SPEED"}'
b'{"SUCCESSFULLY_PROCESSED_COMMAND": "SET_MIN_SPEED"}'
b'{"SUCCESSFULLY_PROCESSED_COMMAND": "LOCK_DOORS"}'
b'{"SUCCESSFULLY_PROCESSED_COMMAND": "TURN_ON_ENGINE"}'
b'{"SUCCESSFULLY_PROCESSED_COMMAND": "ROTATE_RIGHT"}'
```

After you press *Ctrl + C*, you will see an output with a traceback similar to the following lines:

```
^CTraceback (most recent call last):
  File "vehicle_mqtt_remote_control.py", line 86, in <module>
    publish_command(client, CMD_ACCELERATE)
  File "vehicle_mqtt_remote_control.py", line 57, in
    publish_command
    time.sleep(1)
KeyboardInterrupt
```

We interrupted the connection between the MQTT client that works as a remote control for the vehicle and the MQTT server. We didn't wait for all the commands to be published and we disconnected the MQTT client unexpectedly from the MQTT server. The vehicle doesn't know that the remote control application has been interrupted.

In this case, we used a keyboard shortcut to interrupt the execution of the Python program. However, a network failure might be another cause for an unexpected disconnection of the MQTT client from the MQTT server.

Of course, we don't want a network failure to leave our vehicle without control, and therefore, we want to make sure that the vehicle parks in a safe place if the remote control application loses connection with the MQTT server. In this case, we want to make sure the vehicle receives a message with the command that indicates to the vehicle that it must park in a safe place that is configured for the vehicle.

In Chapter 1, *Installing an MQTT 3.1.1 Mosquitto Server*, we analyzed the fields and flags that compose the payload of the CONNECT control packet that an MQTT client sends to an MQTT server to establish a connection. Now, we will use the appropriate method provided in paho-mqtt to configure the values for the Will, WillQoS, WillRetain, WillTopic, and WillMessage flags and fields that will allow our MQTT client to take advantage of the last will and testament feature of MQTT.

Open the existing vehicle_mqtt_remote_control.py Python file and replace the lines that define the __main__ method with the following code to configure the last will message that we want the MQTT server to send to the vehicle if an unexpected disconnection occurs. The added lines are highlighted. The code file for the sample is included in the mqtt_python_gaston_hillar_05_02 folder, in the vehicle_mqtt_remote_control.py file:

```python
if __name__ == "__main__":
    client = mqtt.Client(protocol=mqtt.MQTTv311)
    client.on_connect = on_connect
    client.on_subscribe = on_subscribe
    client.on_message = on_message
    client.tls_set(ca_certs = ca_certificate,
        certfile=client_certificate,
        keyfile=client_key)
    # Set a will to be sent to the MQTT server in case the client
    # disconnects unexpectedly
    last_will_payload = build_command_message(CMD_PARK_IN_SAFE_PLACE)
    client.will_set(topic=commands_topic,
        payload=last_will_payload,
        qos=2)
    client.connect(host=mqtt_server_host,
        port=mqtt_server_port,
        keepalive=mqtt_keepalive)
    publish_command(client, CMD_SET_MAX_SPEED, KEY_MPH, 30)
    publish_command(client, CMD_SET_MIN_SPEED, KEY_MPH, 8)
    publish_command(client, CMD_LOCK_DOORS)
    publish_command(client, CMD_TURN_ON_ENGINE)
    publish_command(client, CMD_ROTATE_RIGHT, KEY_DEGREES, 15)
    publish_command(client, CMD_ACCELERATE)
    publish_command(client, CMD_ROTATE_RIGHT, KEY_DEGREES, 25)
    publish_command(client, CMD_ACCELERATE)
    publish_command(client, CMD_ROTATE_LEFT, KEY_DEGREES, 15)
    publish_command(client, CMD_ACCELERATE)
    publish_command(client, CMD_TURN_OFF_ENGINE)
    while LoopControl.is_last_command_processed == False:
        # Process messages and the commands every 500 milliseconds
        client.loop()
```

```
        time.sleep(0.5)
    client.disconnect()
    client.loop()
```

We added two lines of code before the code calls the `client.connect` method, that is, before we send a connection request to the MQTT server. The first line calls the `build_command_message` function with `CMD_PARK_IN_SAFE_PLACE` as an argument to build the JSON string with the command that makes the vehicle park in a safe place, and stores it in the `last_will_payload` variable.

The next line of code calls the `client.will_set` method that allows us to configure the desired values for the `Will`, `WillQoS`, `WillRetain`, `WillTopic`, and `WillMessage` flags and fields that will be used in the CONNECT control packet. The code calls this method with `commands_topic`, `last_will_payload`, and `2` as the values for the topic, `payload`, and `qos` arguments. As we don't specify a value for the `retain` argument, the method will use its default value, `False`, which specifies that the last will message is not going to be a retained message. This way, when the next line of code calls the `client.connect` method to request the MQTT client to establish a connection to the MQTT server, the CONNECT control packet will include the appropriate values for the fields and flags to configure a last will message with QoS level 2, `commands_topic` as the topic in which the message will be published, and `last_will_payload` as the payload for the message.

Now, execute the following line to start the vehicle remote control example on any computer or device that you want to use as the MQTT client and uses Linux or macOS:

```
python3 vehicle_mqtt_remote_control.py
```

In Windows, you must execute the following line:

```
python vehicle_mqtt_remote_control.py
```

Go to the device and window in which you executed the previous Python script, named `vehicle_mqtt_remote_control.py`. After you see the following output, press *Ctrl + C* to interrupt the execution of the script before all the commands are processed:

```
Result from connect: Connection Accepted.
Subscribed with QoS: 2
b'{"SUCCESSFULLY_PROCESSED_COMMAND": "SET_MAX_SPEED"}'
b'{"SUCCESSFULLY_PROCESSED_COMMAND": "SET_MIN_SPEED"}'
b'{"SUCCESSFULLY_PROCESSED_COMMAND": "LOCK_DOORS"}'
b'{"SUCCESSFULLY_PROCESSED_COMMAND": "TURN_ON_ENGINE"}'
```

After you press *Ctrl + C,* you will see an output with a traceback similar to the following lines:

```
^CTraceback (most recent call last):
    File "vehicle_mqtt_remote_control.py", line 87, in <module>
      publish_command(client, CMD_ROTATE_LEFT, KEY_DEGREES, 15)
    File "vehicle_mqtt_remote_control.py", line 57, in publish_command
      time.sleep(1)
    KeyboardInterrupt
```

We interrupted the connection between the MQTT client that works as a remote control for the vehicle and the MQTT server. We didn't wait for all the commands to be published and we disconnected the MQTT client unexpectedly from the MQTT server. Thus, the MQTT server publishes the configured last will message that the MQTT client, which works as a remote control for the vehicle, has configured when it established a connection with the MQTT server. This way, the vehicle receives a command to park in a safe place when the connection between the remote control application and the MQTT server is lost.

Go to the device and window in which you executed the Python script that controlled the vehicle and processed the received commands, that is, `vehicle_mqtt_client.py`. You will see an output similar to the following lines. Note that the last received message instructs the vehicle to park in a safe place. This last received message is the last will message we configured with the added lines of code in the Python script named `vehicle_mqtt_remote_control.py`:

```
Received message payload: b'{"CMD": "SET_MAX_SPEED", "MPH": 30}'
vehiclepi01: Setting maximum speed to 30 MPH
Received message payload: b'{"CMD": "SET_MIN_SPEED", "MPH": 8}'
vehiclepi01: Setting minimum speed to 8 MPH
Received message payload: b'{"CMD": "LOCK_DOORS"}'
vehiclepi01: Locking doors
Received message payload: b'{"CMD": "TURN_ON_ENGINE"}'
vehiclepi01: Turning on the engine
Received message payload: b'{"CMD": "ROTATE_RIGHT", "DEGREES": 15}'
vehiclepi01: Rotating right 15 degrees
Received message payload: b'{"CMD": "ACCELERATE"}'
vehiclepi01: Accelerating
Received message payload: b'{"CMD": "ROTATE_RIGHT", "DEGREES": 25}'
vehiclepi01: Rotating right 25 degrees
Received message payload: b'{"CMD": "ACCELERATE"}'
vehiclepi01: Accelerating
Received message payload: b'{"CMD": "PARK_IN_SAFE_PLACE"}'
vehiclepi01: Parking in safe place
```

The following screenshot shows two Terminal windows running on a computer with macOS. The Terminal on the left-hand side is displaying the messages shown by the Python client that publishes commands and works as the remote control for the vehicle, that is, the `vehicle_mqtt_remote_control.py` script. The Terminal on the right-hand side is displaying the results of running the code for the Python client that controls the vehicle and processes the received commands, that is, the `vehicle_mqtt_client.py` script. The interruption of the connection generated the MQTT server to publish the configured last will message:

```
(01) Gastons-MacBook-Pro:01 gaston$ python3 vehicle_mqtt_remote_control.py
Result from connect: Connection Accepted.
Subscribed with QoS: 2
b'{"SUCCESSFULLY_PROCESSED_COMMAND": "SET_MAX_SPEED"}'
b'{"SUCCESSFULLY_PROCESSED_COMMAND": "SET_MIN_SPEED"}'
b'{"SUCCESSFULLY_PROCESSED_COMMAND": "LOCK_DOORS"}'
b'{"SUCCESSFULLY_PROCESSED_COMMAND": "TURN_ON_ENGINE"}'
^CTraceback (most recent call last):
  File "vehicle_mqtt_remote_control.py", line 87, in <module>
    publish_command(client, CMD_ROTATE_LEFT, KEY_DEGREES, 15)
  File "vehicle_mqtt_remote_control.py", line 57, in publish_command
    time.sleep(1)
KeyboardInterrupt
(01) Gastons-MacBook-Pro:01 gaston$
```

```
(01) Gastons-MacBook-Pro:01 gaston$ python3 vehicle_mqtt_client.py
Result from connect: Connection Accepted.
Received message payload: b'{"CMD": "SET_MAX_SPEED", "MPH": 30}'
vehiclepi01: Setting maximum speed to 30 MPH
Received message payload: b'{"CMD": "SET_MIN_SPEED", "MPH": 8}'
vehiclepi01: Setting minimum speed to 8 MPH
Received message payload: b'{"CMD": "LOCK_DOORS"}'
vehiclepi01: Locking doors
Received message payload: b'{"CMD": "TURN_ON_ENGINE"}'
vehiclepi01: Turning on the engine
Received message payload: b'{"CMD": "ROTATE_RIGHT", "DEGREES": 15}'
vehiclepi01: Rotating right 15 degrees
Received message payload: b'{"CMD": "ACCELERATE"}'
vehiclepi01: Accelerating
Received message payload: b'{"CMD": "ROTATE_RIGHT", "DEGREES": 25}'
vehiclepi01: Rotating right 25 degrees
Received message payload: b'{"CMD": "ACCELERATE"}'
vehiclepi01: Accelerating
Received message payload: b'{"CMD": "PARK_IN_SAFE_PLACE"}'
vehiclepi01: Parking in safe place
```

> You can take advantage of the last will and testament feature to indicate to interested clients that a specific board, device, or sensor is offline.

Now, execute the following line to start the vehicle remote control example on any computer or device that you want to use as the MQTT client and uses Linux or macOS:

```
python3 vehicle_mqtt_remote_control.py
```

In Windows, you must execute the following line:

```
python vehicle_mqtt_remote_control.py
```

Go to the device and window in which you executed the previous Python script, named `vehicle_mqtt_remote_control.py`.

This time, keep the code running on your local computer or on the IoT board you have chosen to use as the vehicle remote control for this example.

Go to the device and window in which you executed the Python script that controlled the vehicle and processed the received commands, that is, `vehicle_mqtt_client.py`. You will see the following last lines in the output:

```
Received message payload: b'{"CMD": "ROTATE_LEFT", "DEGREES": 15}'
vehiclepi01: Rotating left 15 degrees
Received message payload: b'{"CMD": "ACCELERATE"}'
vehiclepi01: Accelerating
Received message payload: b'{"CMD": "TURN_OFF_ENGINE"}'
vehiclepi01: Turning off the engine
```

In this case, the code called the `client.disconnect` method and then the `client.loop` method. The MQTT client disconnected from the MQTT server in a normal way, and therefore, the last will message with the command to park the vehicle in a safe place wasn't published.

It is very important to understand that the configured last will message isn't published when the MQTT client disconnects from the MQTT by calling the `client.disconnect` method and making sure that the network events are processed. If we want to publish a message before a normal disconnection performed with the `client.disconnect` method, we must write the necessary code to do so before calling this method. In addition, we have to make sure that the network events are processed.

Working with retained last will messages

Now, we will check what happens when the MQTT client that controls the vehicle disconnects unexpectedly from the MQTT server and our vehicle remote control application disconnects unexpectedly, too. Pay attention to all the steps because we will manually interrupt the execution of both programs to understand a specific problem that we will solve by taking advantage of the last will and testament feature combined with the retained flag value.

You will have to be quick to run the next steps. Hence, make sure you read all the steps and then execute them.

Execute the following line to start the vehicle remote control example on any computer or device that you want to use as the MQTT client and uses Linux or macOS:

```
python3 vehicle_mqtt_remote_control.py
```

In Windows, you must execute the following line:

```
python vehicle_mqtt_remote_control.py
```

Go to the device and window in which you executed the Python script that controlled the vehicle and processed the received commands, that is, `vehicle_mqtt_client.py`. After you see the following output, press *Ctrl + C* to interrupt the execution of the script before all the commands are received:

```
Received message payload: b'{"CMD": "PARK_IN_SAFE_PLACE"}'
vehiclepi01: Parking in safe place
Received message payload: b'{"CMD": "SET_MAX_SPEED", "MPH": 30}'
vehiclepi01: Setting maximum speed to 30 MPH
```

After you press *Ctrl + C*, you will see an output with a traceback similar to the following lines:

```
^CTraceback (most recent call last):
  File "vehicle_mqtt_client.py", line 198, in <module>
    time.sleep(1)
    KeyboardInterrupt
```

We interrupted the connection between the MQTT client that controls the vehicle and processes the received commands and the MQTT server. We didn't wait for all the commands to be received and we disconnected the MQTT client unexpectedly from the MQTT server. The vehicle remote control application doesn't know that the remote control application has been interrupted and it waits until the last command it sent is processed.

Go to the device and window in which you executed the previous Python script, named `vehicle_mqtt_remote_control.py`. Press *Ctrl + C* to interrupt the execution of the script. After you press *Ctrl + C*, you will see an output with a traceback similar to the following lines:

```
^CTraceback (most recent call last):
  File "vehicle_mqtt_remote_control.py", line 93, in <module>
    client.loop()
  File "/Users/gaston/HillarMQTT/01/lib/python3.6/site-
    packages/paho/mqtt/client.py", line 988, in loop
    socklist = select.select(rlist, wlist, [], timeout)
    KeyboardInterrupt
```

Go back to the device and window in which you executed the Python script that controlled the vehicle and processed the received commands, that is, `vehicle_mqtt_client.py`. Execute the following line to start this script again on any computer or device that you want to use as the MQTT client and uses Linux or macOS:

```
python3 vehicle_mqtt_client.py
```

In Windows, you must execute the following line:

```
python vehicle_mqtt_client.py
```

Wait a few seconds and you will only see the following output that indicates the connection to the MQTT server has been accepted. No commands have been received:

```
Result from connect: Connection Accepted.
```

The following screenshot shows two Terminal windows running on a computer with macOS. The Terminal on the left-hand side is displaying the messages shown by the Python client that publishes commands and works as the remote control for the vehicle, that is, the `vehicle_mqtt_remote_control.py` script. The Terminal on the right-hand side is displaying the results of running the code for the Python client that controls the vehicle and processes the received commands, that is, the `vehicle_mqtt_client.py` script after the previously explained interruptions:

When we started the `vehicle_mqtt_client.py` script, the code generated a new MQTT client and established a connection with the MQTT server and subscribed to `vehicles/vehiclepi01/commands`. The last will message published to this topic when we interrupted the execution of the `vehicle_mqtt_remote_control.py` script had been published with the `Retained` flag set to `False`, therefore, the message wasn't retained by the MQTT server and any new subscription to a topic filter that matches the topic to which the retained last will message has been sent doesn't receive it.

Open the existing `vehicle_mqtt_remote_control.py` Python file and replace the lines that call the `client.will_set` method within the `__main__` method with the following code. The code file for the sample is included in the `mqtt_python_gaston_hillar_05_03` folder, in the `vehicle_mqtt_remote_control.py` file:

```
client.will_set(topic=commands_topic,
    payload=last_will_payload,
    qos=2,
    retain=True)
```

We specified the `True` value for the `retain` argument that, in the previous version of the code, used the default `False` value. This way, the last will message is going to be a retained message.

Execute the following line to start the vehicle remote control example on any computer or device that you want to use as the MQTT client and uses Linux or macOS:

```
python3 vehicle_mqtt_remote_control.py
```

In Windows, you must execute the following line:

```
python vehicle_mqtt_remote_control.py
```

Go to the device and window in which you executed the Python script that controlled the vehicle and processed the received commands, that is, `vehicle_mqtt_client.py`. After you see the following output, press *Ctrl + C* to interrupt the execution of the script before all the commands are received:

```
Received message payload: b'{"CMD": "PARK_IN_SAFE_PLACE"}'
vehiclepi01: Parking in safe place
```

After you press *Ctrl + C*, you will see an output with a traceback similar to the following lines:

```
^CTraceback (most recent call last):
  File "vehicle_mqtt_client.py", line 198, in <module>
    time.sleep(1)
  KeyboardInterrupt
```

We interrupted the connection between the MQTT client that controls the vehicle and processes the received commands and the MQTT server. We didn't wait for all the commands to be received and we disconnected the MQTT client unexpectedly from the MQTT server. The vehicle remote control application doesn't know that the remote control application has been interrupted and it waits until the last command it sent is processed.

Go to the device and window in which you executed the previous Python script, named `vehicle_mqtt_remote_control.py`. Press *Ctrl + C* to interrupt the execution of the script. After you press *Ctrl + C*, you will see an output with a traceback similar to the following lines:

```
^CTraceback (most recent call last):
  File "vehicle_mqtt_remote_control.py", line 93, in <module>
    client.loop()
  File "/Users/gaston/HillarMQTT/01/lib/python3.6/site-
packages/paho/mqtt/client.py", line 988, in loop
    socklist = select.select(rlist, wlist, [], timeout)
    KeyboardInterrupt
```

Go back to the device and window in which you executed the Python script that controlled the vehicle and processed the received commands, that is, `vehicle_mqtt_client.py`. Execute the following line to start this script again on any computer or device that you want to use as the MQTT client and uses Linux or macOS:

```
python3 vehicle_mqtt_client.py
```

In Windows, you must execute the following line:

```
python vehicle_mqtt_client.py
```

Wait a few seconds and you will only see the output which indicates the connection to the MQTT server has been accepted, and a message, which indicates the retained last will message that instructs the vehicle to park in a safe place has been received and processed. Hence, the vehicle will be parked in a safe place:

```
Result from connect: Connection Accepted.
Received message payload: b'{"CMD": "PARK_IN_SAFE_PLACE"}'
vehiclepi01: Parking in safe place
```

The following screenshot shows two Terminal windows running on a computer with macOS. The Terminal on the left-hand side is displaying the messages shown by the Python client that publishes commands and works as the remote control for the vehicle, that is, the `vehicle_mqtt_remote_control.py` script. The Terminal on the right-hand side is displaying the results of running the code for the Python client that controls the vehicle and processes the received commands, that is, the `vehicle_mqtt_client.py` script after the previously explained interruptions:

With the new code, when we started the `vehicle_mqtt_client.py` script, the code generated a new MQTT client, established a connection with the MQTT server, and subscribed to the `vehicles/vehiclepi01/commands`. The last will message published to this topic when we interrupted the execution of the `vehicle_mqtt_remote_control.py` script had been published with the `Retained` flag set to `True`, and therefore, the message was retained by the MQTT server and any new subscription to a topic filter that matches the topic to which the retained last will message has been sent receives it. The retained last will message allows us to make sure that the message arrives as the first message when a new connection to the MQTT server subscribes to a matching topic.

In this case, we always want to make sure that the vehicle receives the last will message if the MQTT client created in the `vehicle_mqtt_client.py` script loses the connection with the MQTT server and then establishes a new connection.

Understanding blocking and non-blocking code

So far, we have been working with blocking calls that processed MQTT-related network traffic and dispatched callbacks. Whenever we called the `client.loop` method in the previous examples, the method used the default values for the two optional arguments: 1 for `timeout` and 1 for `max_packets`. The method blocks for up to one second, that is, the value of the `timeout` argument, to handle incoming or outgoing data. The method runs with a synchronous execution, and therefore, the next line of code won't be executed until this method returns. We called the `client.loop` method in the main thread, and therefore, no other code can be executed in this thread while the `client.loop` method is blocking.

In our first example with Python code that created an MQTT client, we called the `client.loop_forever` method. This method blocks until the client calls the `disconnect` method. The method runs with a synchronous execution, and therefore, the next line of code won't be executed until the client calls the `disconnect` method. We also called the `client.loop_forever` in the main thread, and therefore, no other code can be executed in this thread while the `client.loop_forever` method is blocking.

> One important difference between the loop method and the `loop_forever` method is that it is necessary to handle reconnections manually when we work with the loop method. The `loop_forever` method automatically handles reconnections to the MQTT server.

The `paho-mqtt` library provides us with a threaded client interface for the network loop that launches another thread that automatically calls the `loop` method. This way, it is possible to free up the main thread to run other code. The threaded interface is non-blocking and we don't have to worry about repeatedly calling the `loop` method. In addition, the threaded interface automatically handles reconnections to the MQTT server.

Using the threaded client interface

Now, we will write a new version of the vehicle remote control application to use the threaded interface, also known as the threaded loop. Open the existing `vehicle_mqtt_remote_control.py` Python file and replace the lines that define the `publish_command` function with the following lines. The code file for the sample is included in the `mqtt_python_gaston_hillar_05_04` folder, in the `vehicle_mqtt_remote_control.py` file:

```
def publish_command(client, command_name, key="", value=""):
    command_message = build_command_message(
        command_name, key, value)
    result = client.publish(topic=commands_topic,
    payload=command_message, qos=2)
    time.sleep(1)
    return result
```

We removed the following line before the call to `time.sleep(1)`:

```
client.loop()
```

The threaded loop will automatically call `client.loop` in another thread, and therefore, we don't need to include a call to `client.loop` within the `publish_command` method anymore.

Open the existing `vehicle_mqtt_remote_control.py` Python file and replace the lines that define the `__main__` method with the following code to use the threaded loop. The added lines are highlighted. The code file for the sample is included in the `mqtt_python_gaston_hillar_05_04` folder, in the `vehicle_mqtt_remote_control.py` file:

```
if __name__ == "__main__":
    client = mqtt.Client(protocol=mqtt.MQTTv311)
    client.on_connect = on_connect
    client.on_subscribe = on_subscribe
    client.on_message = on_message
    client.tls_set(ca_certs = ca_certificate,
        certfile=client_certificate,
        keyfile=client_key)
    # Set a will to be sent to the MQTT server in case the client
    # disconnects unexpectedly
    last_will_payload = build_command_message(CMD_PARK_IN_SAFE_PLACE)
    client.will_set(topic=commands_topic,
        payload=last_will_payload,
        qos=2,
```

```
        retain=True)
    client.connect(host=mqtt_server_host,
        port=mqtt_server_port,
        keepalive=mqtt_keepalive)
    client.loop_start()
    publish_command(client, CMD_SET_MAX_SPEED, KEY_MPH, 30)
    publish_command(client, CMD_SET_MIN_SPEED, KEY_MPH, 8)
    publish_command(client, CMD_LOCK_DOORS)
    publish_command(client, CMD_TURN_ON_ENGINE)
    publish_command(client, CMD_ROTATE_RIGHT, KEY_DEGREES, 15)
    publish_command(client, CMD_ACCELERATE)
    publish_command(client, CMD_ROTATE_RIGHT, KEY_DEGREES, 25)
    publish_command(client, CMD_ACCELERATE)
    publish_command(client, CMD_ROTATE_LEFT, KEY_DEGREES, 15)
    publish_command(client, CMD_ACCELERATE)
    publish_command(client, CMD_TURN_OFF_ENGINE)
    while LoopControl.is_last_command_processed == False:
        # Check whether the last command has been processed or not
        # every 500 milliseconds
        time.sleep(0.5)
    client.disconnect()
    client.loop_stop()
```

After calling the `client.connect` method, the code calls the `client.loop_start` method. This method starts a new thread that processes the MQTT network traffic and frees up the main thread.

Then, the calls to the edited `publish_command` function do not call `client.loop` anymore because the threaded client interface that we started with `client.loop_start` will automatically call the loop to process outgoing messages.

The `while` loop that checks whether the last command has been processed or not every 500 milliseconds doesn't call `client.loop` anymore. Now, there is another thread that is calling `client.loop` for us.

When the last command is processed, the code calls the `client.disconnect` method and finally calls the `client.loop_stop` method to stop the thread that is running the threaded client interface. This method will return when the thread is finished.

Execute the following line to start the new version of the vehicle remote control example on any computer or device that you want to use as the MQTT client and uses Linux or macOS:

```
python3 vehicle_mqtt_remote_control.py
```

In Windows, you must execute the following line:

```
python vehicle_mqtt_remote_control.py
```

You will note that the timing between the send commands and the processed commands is clearer because the time at which the network events are processed is more accurate in the new version.

Test your knowledge

Let's see whether you can answer the following questions correctly:

1. Which of the following methods of the `paho.mqtt.client.Client` instance blocks execution and ensures communication with the MQTT server is carried out?
    1. `loop`
    2. `loop_start`
    3. `blocking_loop`

2. Which of the following methods of the `paho.mqtt.client.Client` instance starts a new thread and ensures communication with the MQTT server is carried out?
    1. `loop`
    2. `loop_start`
    3. `non_blocking_loop`

3. Which of the following methods of the `paho.mqtt.client.Client` instance configures a last will message to be sent to the MQTT server if the client disconnects unexpectedly?
    1. `last_will_publish`
    2. `last_will_message`
    3. `will_set`

4. Which of the following methods of the `paho.mqtt.client.Client` instance stops the thread that is running the threaded client interface?
    1. `loop_end`
    2. `non_blocking_loop_stop`
    3. `loop_stop`

5. Which of the following methods is non-blocking?
    1. `loop_start`
    2. `non_blocking_loop`
    3. `loop_forever`

The right answers are included in the `Appendix`, *Solutions*.

Summary

In this chapter, we processed commands received as JSON strings within MQTT messages with Python code. Then, we coded a Python client that composed and published messages with commands to work as a remote control application for the vehicle controller.

We worked with the blocking network loop and then we converted the application to use the threaded client interface to avoid blocking the main thread. We took advantage of the last will and testament feature to make sure a controlled vehicle parks in a safe place whenever a connection is lost. Then, we worked with retained last will messages.

Now that we understand how to use Python to work with multiple MQTT applications that take advantage of advanced features, we will use a cloud-based real-time MQTT provider to monitor a surfing completion in which we will need to receive and process data from multiple sensors, which is what we are going to discuss in `Chapter 6`, *Monitoring a surfing competition with cloud-based real-time MQTT providers and Python.*

6
Monitoring a Surfing Competition with Cloud-Based Real-Time MQTT Providers and Python

In this chapter, we will write Python code to use the PubNub cloud-based real-time MQTT provider in combination with a Mosquitto MQTT server to monitor a surfing competition. We will build a solution from scratch by analyzing the requirements, and we will write Python code that will run on waterproof IoT boards connected to multiple sensors in surfboards. We will define the topics and commands, and we will work with a cloud-based MQTT server in combination with the Mosquitto MQTT server used in the previous chapters. We will cover the following:

- Understanding the requirements
- Defining the topics and payloads
- Coding a surfboard sensor emulator
- Configuring PubNub MQTT interface
- Publishing data retrieved from sensors to the cloud-based MQTT server
- Working with multiple MQTT servers
- Building a web-based dashboard with freeboard

Understanding the requirements

Many surfers that are training for surfing competitions want us to build a real-time web-based dashboard with the data provided by an IoT board connected to multiple sensors in the surfboards. Each IoT board will provide the following data:

- **Status**: Many wearable wireless sensors embedded in each surfer's wetsuit and other sensors included in the surfboard will provide data and the IoT board will perform a real-time analysis to indicate the status of the surfer
- **Speed**: A sensor will measure the surfboard's speed in **miles per hour** (**mph**)
- **Altitude**: A sensor will measure the surfboard's altitude in feet
- **Water temperature**: A sensor located in one of the surfboard's fins will measure the water temperature in degrees Fahrenheit

Third-party software is running on the IoT board and we cannot make changes to the code that publishes the data on different topics. We can provide the necessary certificates to configure the secured connection with our Mosquitto MQTT server and specify its host name and protocol. In addition, we can configure a name that identifies the surfboard and determines the topics in which the data will be published.

Defining the topics and payloads

The IoT board uses the following topic names to publish data about a specific surfboard, where `surfboardname` must be replaced with a unique name assigned to a surfboard:

Variable	Topic name
Status	`surfboards/surfboardname/status`
Speed (mph)	`surfboards/surfboardname/speedmph`
Altitude (feet)	`surfboards/surfboardname/altitudefeet`
Water temperature (degrees Fahrenheit)	`surfboards/surfboardname/temperaturef`

For example, if we assign `surfboard01` as the name for the surfboard, the client that wants to receive the actual speed for the surfboard has to subscribe to the `surfboards/surfboard01/speedmph` topic.

The IoT board and its connected sensors are capable of distinguishing between the following five possible statuses of a surfer and their surfboard:

Status key	Meaning
0	Idle
1	Paddling
2	Riding
3	Ride finished
4	Wiped out

The IoT board publishes the integer value specified in the status key column that indicates the current status of a surfer and their surfboard. For example, when a surfer is riding a wave, the board will publish 2 to the `surfboards/surfboard01/status` topic.

The board will publish floating-point values in the previously explained topics for speed, altitude, and water temperature. In this case, the IoT board will just publish either the integer or floating-point values as the payloads for the MQTT messages. The payload won't be JSON, as in our previous examples. The payload won't include any additional information about the unit of measurement. This information is included in the topic name.

The IoT board will publish the data in the previously explained topics every second.

In the previous examples, we designed our solution from scratch. In this case, we have to interact with an IoT board that is already running code that we cannot change. Imagine that we have to start working on the solution without the IoT board; therefore, we will develop a surfboard sensor emulator in Python that will provide us with data so that we can receive the published data and develop the desired dashboard. In real-life projects, this is a very common scenario.

As we learned in the previous chapters, MQTT has become an extremely popular protocol for IoT projects in which many sensors have to publish data. Due to this increasing popularity, many cloud-based messaging infrastructures have included MQTT interfaces or bridges. For example, the PubNub data stream network provides a scalable MQTT interface. We can take advantage of everything we learned so far about MQTT to work with this cloud-based data stream network. You can read more about PubNub on its web page: `http://www.pubnub.com`.

A Python program will collect the data published by the IoT board by subscribing to the four topics and the code will build a complete status for the surfer and their surfboard every second. Then, the code will build a JSON message with the status, speed, altitude, and water temperature and it will publish it to a topic of the MQTT PubNub interface.

In our example, we will take advantage of the free services offered by PubNub and its MQTT interface. We won't use some advanced features and additional services that might empower our IoT project connectivity requirements, but also require a paid subscription.

We will take advantage of freeboard.io to visualize the data collected from the sensors and published to the PubNub MQTT interface in many gauges and make the dashboard available to different computers and devices all over the world. freeboard.io allows us to build a dashboard by selecting data sources and dragging and dropping customizable widgets. freeboard.io defines itself as a cloud-based service that allows us to visualize the Internet of Things. You can read more about freeboard.io in its web page: `http://freeboard.io`.

In our example, we will take advantage of the free services offered by freeboard.io and we won't use some advanced features that provide privacy for our dashboards, but also require a paid subscription. Our dashboard will be available to anyone that has the unique URL for it because we are not working with private dashboards.

The following lines show an example of the payload for the message that provides the status of the surfer and their surfboard:

```
{
    "Status": "Riding",
    "Speed MPH": 15.0,
    "Altitude Feet": 3.0,
    "Water Temperature F": 56.0
}
```

Freeboard.io allows us to easily select each key of the JSON message received in the PubNub MQTT interface as a data source for the dashboard. This way, we will easily build a web-based dashboard to provide us with the status, speed, altitude, and water temperature values in gauges.

To summarize, our solution will be composed of the following two Python programs:

- **Surfboard sensor emulator**: This program will establish a secured connection to our Mosquitto MQTT server and it will publish status, speed, altitude, and water temperature values read from a **CSV** (short for **Comma Separated Values**) file to the appropriate topics every second. The program will work as if we had a real-life surfer with his wetsuit and surfboard sensors riding waves and publishing data.

- **Surfboard monitor**: This program will establish a secured connection to our Mosquitto MQTT server and it will subscribe to the topics in which the surfboard sensor emulator publishes status, speed, altitude, and water temperature values. The surfboard monitor program will also establish a connection with the PubNub MQTT interface. The program will publish a single message with the key-value pairs that determine the status of a surfer and their surfboard to the PubNub MQTT interface every second.

Coding a surfboard sensor emulator

First, we will create a CSV file with many status, speed in mph, altitude in feet, and temperature in degrees Fahrenheit values separated by commas. Each line in the file will represent a set of values that the surfboard sensor emulator will publish to the appropriate topics. In this case, it is not convenient to work with random values because we want to emulate real-life scenarios for a surfer and his surfboard.

Now, we will create a new file named `surfboard_sensors_data.csv` in the main virtual environment folder. The following lines show the code that defines the data retrieved from a short surfing session for the surfer and their surfboard.

The values separated with commas from left to right are the following: speed in mph, altitude in feet, and temperature in degrees Fahrenheit. First, the surfer is idle, he increases the speed when paddling, he reaches the speed maximum value when riding the wave, and finally reduces speed when his status is set to ride finished. The code file for the sample is included in the mqtt_python_gaston_hillar_06_01 folder, in the surfboard_sensors_data.csv file:

```
0, 1, 2, 58
0, 1.1, 2, 58
1, 2, 3, 57
1, 3, 3, 57
1, 3, 3, 57
1, 3, 3, 57
1, 4, 4, 57
1, 5, 5, 57
2, 8, 5, 57
2, 10, 4, 57
2, 12, 4, 56
2, 15, 3, 56
2, 15, 3, 56
2, 15, 3, 56
2, 15, 3, 56
2, 15, 3, 56
2, 12, 3, 56
3, 3, 3, 55
3, 2, 3, 55
3, 1, 3, 55
3, 0, 3, 55
```

Now, we will create a new Python file named surfboard_config.py in the main virtual environment folder. The following lines show the code for this file, which defines many configuration values that will be used to configure the topics to which the surfboard sensor emulator will publish the values retrieved from the sensors. The surfboard monitor will also need these topics to subscribe to them, and therefore it is convenient to include all the configuration values in a specific Python script. The code file for the sample is included in the mqtt_python_gaston_hillar_06_01 folder, in the surfboard_config.py file:

```
surfboard_name = "surfboard01"
topic_format = "surfboards/{}/{}"
status_topic = topic_format.format(
    surfboard_name,
    "status")
speed_mph_topic = topic_format.format(
    surfboard_name,
    "speedmph")
altitude_feet_topic = topic_format.format(
```

```
    surfboard_name,
    "altitudefeet")
water_temperature_f_topic = topic_format.format(
    surfboard_name,
    "temperaturef")
```

The code defines the surfboard name and stores it in the `surfboard_name` variable. The `topic_format` variable holds a string that makes it easy to build different topics that have a common prefix. The following table summarizes the string values for the four variables that define the topic names for each sensor, based on a defined surfboard named `surfboard01`:

Variable	Value
status_topic	surfboards/surfboard01/status
speed_mph_topic	surfboards/surfboard01/speedmph
altitude_feet_topic	surfboards/surfboard01/altitudefeet
temperature_f_topic	surfboards/surfboard01/temperaturef

Now, we will create a new Python file named `surfboard_sensors_emulator.py` in the main virtual environment folder. The following lines show the code for this file, which establishes a connection with our Mosquitto MQTT server, reads the previously created `surfboard_sensors_data.csv` CSV file, and continuously publishes the values read from this file to the previously enumerated topics. The code file for the sample is included in the `mqtt_python_gaston_hillar_06_01` folder, in the `surfboard_sensors_emulator.py` file:

```
from config import *
from surfboard_config import *
import paho.mqtt.client as mqtt
import time
import csv


def on_connect(client, userdata, flags, rc):
    print("Result from connect: {}".format(
        mqtt.connack_string(rc)))
    # Check whether the result form connect is the CONNACK_ACCEPTED connack
code
    if rc != mqtt.CONNACK_ACCEPTED:
        raise IOError("I couldn't establish a connection with the MQTT
server")

def publish_value(client, topic, value):
    result = client.publish(topic=topic,
```

```
            payload=value,
            qos=0)
    return result


if __name__ == "__main__":
    client = mqtt.Client(protocol=mqtt.MQTTv311)
    client.on_connect = on_connect
    client.tls_set(ca_certs = ca_certificate,
        certfile=client_certificate,
        keyfile=client_key)
    client.connect(host=mqtt_server_host,
        port=mqtt_server_port,
        keepalive=mqtt_keepalive)
    client.loop_start()
    publish_debug_message = "{}: {}"
    try:
        while True:
            with open('surfboard_sensors_data.csv') as csvfile:
                reader=csv.reader(csvfile)
                for row in reader:
                    status_value = int(row[0])
                    speed_mph_value = float(row[1])
                    altitude_feet_value = float(row[2])
                    water_temperature_f_value = float(row[3])
                    print(publish_debug_message.format(
                        status_topic,
                        status_value))
                    print(publish_debug_message.format(
                        speed_mph_topic,
                        speed_mph_value))
                    print(publish_debug_message.format(
                        altitude_feet_topic,
                        altitude_feet_value))
                    print(publish_debug_message.format(
                        water_temperature_f_topic,
                        water_temperature_f_value))
                    publish_value(client,
                        status_topic,
                        status_value)
                    publish_value(client,
                        speed_mph_topic,
                        speed_mph_value)
                    publish_value(client,
                        altitude_feet_topic,
                        altitude_feet_value)
                    publish_value(client,
                        water_temperature_f_topic,
```

```
                    water_temperature_f_value)
    time.sleep(1)
        except KeyboardInterrupt:
            print("I'll disconnect from the MQTT server")
            client.disconnect()
            client.loop_stop()
```

In Chapter 4, *Writing Code to Control a Vehicle with Python and MQTT Messages*, we created a Python file named config.py in the main virtual environment folder. In this file, we defined many configuration values that were used to establish a connection with the Mosquitto MQTT server. This way, all the configuration values were included in a specific Python script. If you need to make changes to this file to configure the surfboard emulator and the future surfboard monitor, make sure you review the explanations included in that chapter.

The first lines import the variables we have declared in the config.py file and in the previously coded surfboard_config.py file. In this case, we also import the csv module to enable us to easily read from the CSV file that contains the values for the emulated sensors. The code for the on_connect function is very similar to the one we used in our previous examples.

The publish_value function receives the MQTT client, the topic name, and the value that we want to publish in the client, topic, and value arguments. The function calls the client.publish method to publish the received value as the payload to the topic name received in the topic argument with a QoS level of 0.

The main block uses our very well-known code to establish a connection with the Mosquitto MQTT server. After calling the client.connect method, the code calls the client.loop_start method to start a new thread that processes the MQTT network traffic and frees up the main thread.

Then, the codes enters in a continuous loop that opens the `surfboard_sensors_data.csv` CSV file and creates a `csv.reader` to read each row of comma-separated values into the `row` array. The code retrieves the string in `row[0]`, which represents the status value; converts it to an integer value; and saves the value in the `status_value` local variable. The next lines retrieve the strings for speed, altitude, and water temperature in `row[1]`, `row[2]`, and `row[3]`. The code converts these three values to floats and saves them in the `speed_mph_value`, `altitude_feet_value` and `water_temperature_f_value` local variables.

The next lines print debug messages with the values read for each emulated sensor from the CSV file and call the previously explained `publish_value` function for each of these values. Each call to the `publish_value` function uses the appropriate variable for the topic name that was configured in the `surfboard_config.py` file because each value is published to a different topic.

After the code publishes the values for the four emulated sensors, it sleeps for one second and repeats the procedure for the next line in the CSV file. After the last line is read, the code starts the loop again until the user presses *Ctrl + C* and causes a `KeyboardInterrupt` exception to be thrown and captured. In this case, we capture this exception and call the `client.disconnect` and `client.loop_stop` methods to have an appropriate disconnection from the Mosquitto MQTT server. In previous examples, we didn't care about this exception.

Configuring the PubNub MQTT interface

PubNub requires us to sign up and create an account with a valid email and a password before we can create an application in PubNub, which allows us to start using their free services, including the PubNub MQTT interface for a device. We aren't required to enter any credit card or payment information. If you already have an account at PubNub, you can skip the next step.

Once you have created your account, PubNub will redirect you to the admin portal that lists your PubNub applications. It is necessary to generate your PubNub publish and subscribe keys in order to send and receive messages on the network. Click on **CREATE NEW APP+**, enter `MQTT` in **App Name**, and click **CREATE**.

A new pane will represent the application in the admin portal. The following screenshot shows the MQTT application pane in the PubNub admin portal:

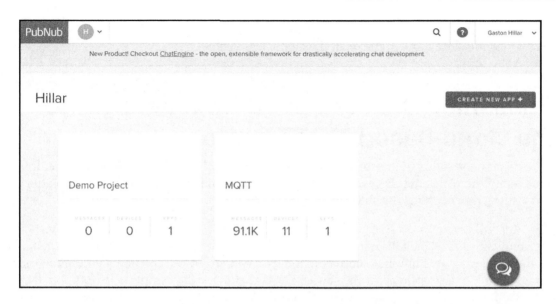

Click on the **MQTT** pane and PubNub will display the **Demo Keyset** pane, which has been automatically generated for the application. Click on this pane and PubNub will display the **Publish Key**, **Subscribe Key**, and **Secret key**. We must copy and paste each of these keys to use them in our code that will use the PubNub MQTT interface to publish messages and the freeboard.io web-based dashboard that will subscribe to them. The following screenshot shows the prefixes for the keys. Notice that the remaining characters have been erased in the image:

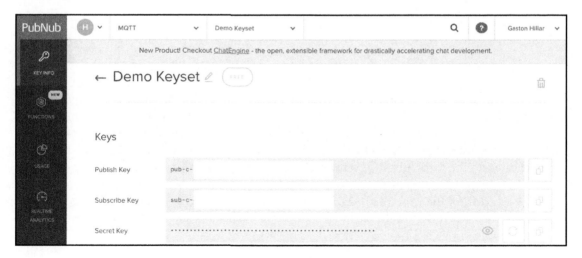

In order to copy the **Secret key**, you must click on the eye icon at the right-hand side of the **Secret key** and PubNub will make all the characters visible.

Publishing data retrieved from sensors to the cloud-based MQTT server

If we display the status of the surfer and his surfboard with numbers, it will be difficult to understand the real status. So, we will have to map the integer that represents the status into a string that explains the status.

Now, we will create a new Python file named `surfboard_status.py` in the main virtual environment folder. The following lines show the code for this file, which defines constants for the different status numbers and a dictionary that maps these constants with integers to strings with the descriptions for the status. The code file for the sample is included in the `mqtt_python_gaston_hillar_06_01` folder, in the `surfboard_status.py` file:

```
SURFBOARD_STATUS_IDLE = 0
SURFBOARD_STATUS_PADDLING = 1
SURFBOARD_STATUS_RIDING = 2
SURFBOARD_STATUS_RIDE_FINISHED = 3
SURFBOARD_STATUS_WIPED_OUT = 4

SURFBOARD_STATUS_DICTIONARY = {
    SURFBOARD_STATUS_IDLE: 'Idle',
    SURFBOARD_STATUS_PADDLING: 'Paddling',
    SURFBOARD_STATUS_RIDING: 'Riding',
    SURFBOARD_STATUS_RIDE_FINISHED: 'Ride finished',
    SURFBOARD_STATUS_WIPED_OUT: 'Wiped out',
    }
```

Now, we will write the code for the surfboard monitor. We will split the code into many code snippets to make it easier to understand each code section. Create a new Python file named `surfboard_monitor.py` in the main virtual environment folder. The following lines declare all the necessary imports and the variables that we will use to establish a connection with the PubNub MQTT interface. Don't forget to replace the strings assigned to the `pubnub_publish_key` and `pubnub_subscribe_key` variables with the values you have retrieved from the previously explained PubNub key generation process. The code file for the sample is included in the `mqtt_python_gaston_hillar_06_01` folder, in the `surfboard_monitor.py` file:

```
from config import *
```

```
from surfboard_status import *
from surfboard_config import *
import paho.mqtt.client as mqtt
import time
import json


# Publish key is the one that usually starts with the "pub-c-" prefix
# Do not forget to replace the string with your publish key
pubnub_publish_key = "pub-c-xxxxxxxx-xxxx-xxxx-xxxx-xxxxxxxxxxxx"
# Subscribe key is the one that usually starts with the "sub-c" prefix
# Do not forget to replace the string with your subscribe key
pubnub_subscribe_key = "sub-c-xxxxxxxx-xxxx-xxxx-xxxx-xxxxxxxxxxxx"
pubnub_mqtt_server_host = "mqtt.pndsn.com"
pubnub_mqtt_server_port = 1883
pubnub_mqtt_keepalive = 60
device_id = surfboard_name
pubnub_topic = surfboard_name
```

The first lines import the variables we have declared in the config.py file and in the previously coded surfboard_config.py and surfboard_status.py files. Then, the code declares the following variables that we will use to establish a connection with the PubNub MQTT interface:

- pubnub_publish_key: This string specifies the PubNub publish key.
- pubnub_subscribe_key: This string specifies the PubNub subscribe key.
- pubnub_mqtt_server_host: This string specifies the PubNub MQTT server address. In order to use the PubNub MQTT interface, we must always establish a connection with the mqtt.pndsn.com host.
- pubnub_mqtt_server_port: This number specifies the PubNub MQTT server port. In this case, we will establish an unsecured connection with the PubNub MQTT server, and therefore we will use port number 1883. We want to keep the PubNub MQTT interface configuration simple for this example, and therefore we won't use TLS.
- pubnub_mqtt_keepalive: This number specifies the keep alive interval configuration for the connection with the PubNub MQTT interface.
- device_id: This string specifies the device identifier we want to use when we create an instance of the Surfboard class. The code assigns the surfboard_name value imported from the surfboard_config.py file. We will analyze the code for this class later.

- `Pubnub_topic`: This string specifies the topic to which the surfboard monitor will publish the JSON payload with the key-value pairs that specify the status for the surfer and their surfboard. The code assigns the `surfboard_name` value imported from the `surfboard_config.py` file.

 The surfboard monitor will establish a connection to the `mqtt.pndsn.com` host on port `1883`. So, we have to make sure that our firewall configuration has the appropriate inbound and outbound rules configurations to allow a connection on the specified port.

Add the following lines to the existing `surfboard_monitor.py` in the main virtual environment folder. The following lines declare the `Surfboard` class. The code file for the sample is included in the `mqtt_python_gaston_hillar_06_01` folder, in the `surfboard_monitor.py` file:

```python
class Surfboard:
    active_instance = None
    def __init__(self, device_id, status,
        speed_mph, altitude_feet, water_temperature_f):
        self.device_id = device_id
        self.status = status
        self.speed_mph = speed_mph
        self.altitude_feet = altitude_feet
        self.water_temperature_f = water_temperature_f
        self.is_pubnub_connected = False
        Surfboard.active_instance = self

    def build_json_message(self):
        # Build a message with the status for the surfboard
        message = {
            "Status": SURFBOARD_STATUS_DICTIONARY[self.status],
            "Speed MPH": self.speed_mph,
            "Altitude Feet": self.altitude_feet,
            "Water Temperature F": self.water_temperature_f,
        }
        json_message = json.dumps(message)
        return json_message
```

We have to specify a `device_id` and the initial values for the data that the sensors provide in the `device_id`, `status`, `speed_mph`, `altitude_feet`, and `water_temperature_f` required arguments. The constructor, that is, the __init__ method, saves the received values in attributes with the same names.

The code also saves a reference to this instance in the `active_instance` class attribute because we have to access the instance in many functions that we will specify as callbacks for the different events that two MQTT clients will fire: the PubNub MQTT client and the Mosquitto MQTT client. We will access the active instance with the `Surfboard.active_instance` class attribute after the code creates a `Surfboard` instance.

The class declares the `build_json_message` method, which builds a message with the status for the surfboard and returns the JSON string with the key-value pairs that composes the status message. The code maps the number stored in the `status` attribute into the string that explains the status by using the `SURFBOARD_STATUS_DICTIONARY` declared in the `surfboard_status.py` file. The code uses the `speed_mph`, `altitude_feet`, and `water_temperature_f` attributes to provide the values for the other keys.

Add the following lines to the existing `surfboard_monitor.py` in the main virtual environment folder. The following lines declare the functions that we will use as callbacks and other functions that will be called by these callbacks. The code file for the sample is included in the `mqtt_python_gaston_hillar_06_01` folder, in the `surfboard_monitor.py` file:

```
def on_connect_mosquitto(client, userdata, flags, rc):
    print("Result from Mosquitto connect: {}".format(
        mqtt.connack_string(rc)))
    # Check whether the result form connect is the CONNACK_ACCEPTED connack
code
    if rc == mqtt.CONNACK_ACCEPTED:
        # Subscribe to a topic filter that provides all the sensors
        sensors_topic_filter = topic_format.format(
            surfboard_name,
            "+")
        client.subscribe(sensors_topic_filter, qos=0)


def on_subscribe_mosquitto(client, userdata, mid, granted_qos):
    print("I've subscribed with QoS: {}".format(
        granted_qos[0]))


def print_received_message_mosquitto(msg):
    print("Message received. Topic: {}. Payload: {}".format(
```

```
                msg.topic,
                str(msg.payload)))


    def on_status_message_mosquitto(client, userdata, msg):
        print_received_message_mosquitto(msg)
        Surfboard.active_instance.status = int(msg.payload)


    def on_speed_mph_message_mosquitto(client, userdata, msg):
        print_received_message_mosquitto(msg)
        Surfboard.active_instance.speed_mph = float(msg.payload)


    def on_altitude_feet_message_mosquitto(client, userdata, msg):
        print_received_message_mosquitto(msg)
        Surfboard.active_instance.altitude_feet = float(msg.payload)


    def on_water_temperature_f_message_mosquitto(client, userdata, msg):
        print_received_message_mosquitto(msg)
        Surfboard.active_instance.water_temperature_f = float(msg.payload)


    def on_connect_pubnub(client, userdata, flags, rc):
        print("Result from PubNub connect: {}".format(
            mqtt.connack_string(rc)))
        # Check whether the result form connect is the CONNACK_ACCEPTED connack
code
        if rc == mqtt.CONNACK_ACCEPTED:
            Surfboard.active_instance.is_pubnub_connected = True


    def on_disconnect_pubnub(client, userdata, rc):
        Surfboard.active_instance.is_pubnub_connected = False
        print("Disconnected from PubNub")
```

The code declares the following functions that end with the `mosquitto` prefix:

- `on_connect_mosquitto`: This function is the callback that will be executed once a successful connection has been established with the Mosquitto MQTT server. The code checks the value of the `rc` argument that provides the CONNACK code returned by the Mosquitto MQTT server. If this value matches `mqtt.CONNACK_ACCEPTED`, it means that the Mosquitto MQTT server accepted the connection request, and therefore the code calls the `client.subscribe` method for the MQTT client received in the `client` argument to subscribe to the `surfboards/surfboard01/+` topic filter with a QoS level of 0. This way, the MQTT client will receive the messages sent to the `surfboards/surfboard01/status, surfboards/surfboard01/speedmph, surfboards/surfboard01/altitudefeet`, and `surfboards/surfboard01/temperaturef` topics with the values retrieved from the different sensors.

- `on_subscribe_mosquitto`: This function will be called when the subscription to the `surfboards/surfboard01/+` topic filter has been successfully completed. As in previous examples, the function prints a message indicating the QoS level granted to the subscription.

- `print_received_message_mosquitto`: This function receives an `mqtt.MQTTMessage` instance in the `msg` argument and prints the topic and the payload of this message to help us understand what is happening in the application.

- `on_status_message_mosquitto`: This function will be called when a message to the `surfboards/surfboard01/status` topic arrives from the Mosquitto MQTT server. The function calls the `print_received_message_mosquitto` function with the received `mqtt.MQTTMessage` instance as an argument and sets the value of the `status` attribute of the `Surfboard` active instance to the conversion of the received message's payload to an `int`.

- `on_speed_mph_message_mosquitto`: This function will be called when a message to the `surfboards/surfboard01/speedmph` topic arrives from the Mosquitto MQTT server. The function calls the `print_received_message_mosquitto` function with the received `mqtt.MQTTMessage` instance as an argument and sets the value of the `speed_mph` attribute of the `Surfboard` active instance to the conversion of the received message's payload to a `float`.

- `on_altitude_feet_message_mosquitto`: This function will be called when a message to the `surfboards/surfboard01/altitudefeet` topic arrives from the Mosquitto MQTT server. The function calls the `print_received_message_mosquitto` function with the received `mqtt.MQTTMessage` instance as an argument and sets the value of the `altitude_feet` attribute of the `Surfboard` active instance to the conversion of the received message's payload to an `int`.

- `on_water_temperature_f_message_mosquitto`: This function will be called when a message to the `surfboards/surfboard01/watertemperaturef` topic arrives from the Mosquitto MQTT server. The function calls the `print_received_message_mosquitto` function with the received `mqtt.MQTTMessage` instance as an argument and sets the value of the `water_temperature_f` attribute of the `Surfboard` active instance to the conversion of the received message's payload to an `int`.

In this case, we don't have a single function that works as a callback to process all the incoming messages from the Mosquitto MQTT server. We work with a callback for each specific topic. This way, we don't have to check the topic for the message to determine the code that we have to run.

The code declares the following functions that end with the `pubnub` prefix:

- `on_connect_pubnub`: This function is the callback that will be executed once a successful connection has been established with the PubNub MQTT server. The code checks the value of the `rc` argument that provides the CONNACK code returned by the PubNub MQTT server. If this value matches `mqtt.CONNACK_ACCEPTED`, it means that the PubNub MQTT server accepted the connection request, and therefore the code sets the value of the `is_pubnub_connected` attribute of the Surfboard active instance to `True`.

- `on_disconnect_pubnub`: This function is the callback that will be executed if the client that was connected to the PubNub MQTT server loses the connection. The code sets the value of the `is_pubnub_connected` attribute of the Surfboard active instance to `False` and prints a message.

Working with multiple MQTT servers

Add the following lines to the existing `surfboard_monitor.py` in the main virtual
environment folder. The following lines declare the main block. The code file for the sample
is included in the `mqtt_python_gaston_hillar_06_01` folder, in the
`surfboard_monitor.py` file:

```
if __name__ == "__main__":
    surfboard = Surfboard(device_id=device_id,
        status=SURFBOARD_STATUS_IDLE,
        speed_mph=0,
        altitude_feet=0,
        water_temperature_f=0)
    pubnub_client_id = "{}/{}/{}".format(
        pubnub_publish_key,
        pubnub_subscribe_key,
        device_id)
    pubnub_client = mqtt.Client(client_id=pubnub_client_id,
        protocol=mqtt.MQTTv311)
    pubnub_client.on_connect = on_connect_pubnub
    pubnub_client.on_disconnect = on_disconnect_pubnub
    pubnub_client.connect(host=pubnub_mqtt_server_host,
        port=pubnub_mqtt_server_port,
        keepalive=pubnub_mqtt_keepalive)
    pubnub_client.loop_start()
    mosquitto_client = mqtt.Client(protocol=mqtt.MQTTv311)
    mosquitto_client.on_connect = on_connect_mosquitto
    mosquitto_client.on_subscribe = on_subscribe_mosquitto
    mosquitto_client.message_callback_add(
        status_topic,
        on_status_message_mosquitto)
    mosquitto_client.message_callback_add(
        speed_mph_topic,
        on_speed_mph_message_mosquitto)
    mosquitto_client.message_callback_add(
        altitude_feet_topic,
        on_altitude_feet_message_mosquitto)
    mosquitto_client.message_callback_add(
        water_temperature_f_topic,
        on_water_temperature_f_message_mosquitto)
    mosquitto_client.tls_set(ca_certs = ca_certificate,
        certfile=client_certificate,
        keyfile=client_key)
    mosquitto_client.connect(host=mqtt_server_host,
        port=mqtt_server_port,
        keepalive=mqtt_keepalive)
```

```
mosquitto_client.loop_start()
try:
    while True:
        if Surfboard.active_instance.is_pubnub_connected:
            payload = Surfboard.active_instance.build_json_message()
            result = pubnub_client.publish(topic=pubnub_topic,
                payload=payload,
                qos=0)
            print("Publishing: {}".format(payload))
        else:
            print("Not connected")
        time.sleep(1)
except KeyboardInterrupt:
    print("I'll disconnect from both Mosquitto and PubNub")
    pubnub_client.disconnect()
    pubnub_client.loop_stop()
    mosquitto_client.disconnect()
    mosquitto_client.loop_stop()
```

First, the main block creates an instance of the `Surfboard` class and saves it in the `surfboard` local variable. Then, the code generates the client ID string that is required to establish a connection with the PubNub MQTT interface and saves it in the `pubnub_client_id` local variable. The PubNub MQTT interface requires us to use a client ID composed as follows:

```
publish_key/subscribe_key/device_id
```

The code uses the values of the `pubnub_publish_key`, `pubnub_subscribe_key`, and `device_id` variables to build a client ID as required by the PubNub MQTT interface. Then, the code creates an instance of the `mqtt.Client` class (`paho.mqtt.client.Client`) named `pubnub_client`, which represents the PubNub MQTT interface client. We use this instance to communicate with the PubNub MQTT server.

Then, the code assigns functions to attributes. The following table summarizes these assignments:

Attribute	Assigned function
pubnub_client.on_connect	on_connect_pubnub
pubnub_client.on_disconnect	on_disconnect_pubnub

Then, the code calls the `pubnub_client.connect` method and specifies the values for the `host`, `port`, and `keepalive` arguments. This way, the code asks the MQTT client to establish a connection to the specified PubNub MQTT server. After calling the `pubnub_client.connect` method, the code calls the `pubnub_client.loop_start` method. This method starts a new thread that processes the MQTT network traffic related to the PubNub MQTT interface and frees up the main thread.

Then, the main block creates another instance of the `mqtt.Client` class (`paho.mqtt.client.Client`) named `mosquitto_client`, which represents the Mosquitto MQTT server client. We use this instance to communicate with the local Mosquitto MQTT server.

Then, the code assigns functions to attributes. The following table summarizes these assignments:

Attribute	Assigned function
`mosquitto_client.on_connect`	`on_connect_mosquitto`
`mosquitto_client.on_subscribe`	`on_subscribe_mosquitto`

Notice that in this case, the code doesn't assign a function to `mosquitto_client.on_message`. The next lines call the `mosquitto_client.message_callback_add` method to specify the callback function that the client has to call when it receives a message in a specific topic. The following table summarizes the function that will be called based on the variable that defines the topic in which the message arrives:

Topic variable	Assigned function
`status_topic`	`on_status_message_mosquitto`
`speed_mph_topic`	`on_speed_mph_message_mosquitto`
`altitude_feet_topic`	`on_altitude_feet_message_mosquitto`
`water_temperature_f_topic`	`on_water_temperature_f_message_mosquitto`

Whenever the client receives a message from any of the sensors, it will update the appropriate attribute for the `Surfboard` active instance. These assigned functions are responsible for updating the status of the `Surfboard` active instance.

Then, the code calls the well-known `mosquitto_client.tls_set` and `mosquitto_client.connect` methods. This way, the code asks the MQTT client to establish a connection to the specified Mosquitto MQTT server. After calling the `mosquitto_client.connect` method, the code calls the `mosquitto_client.loop_start` method. This method starts a new thread that processes the MQTT network traffic related to the Mosquitto MQTT server and frees up the main thread.

 Notice that we made two calls to `loop_start`, and therefore we will have two threads processing MQTT network traffic: one for the PubNub MQTT server and the other for the Mosquitto MQTT server.

The next lines declare a `while` loop that runs forever until a `KeyboardInterrupt` exception occurs. The loop checks the value of the `Surfboard.active_instance.is_pubnub_connected` attribute to make sure that the connection to the PubNub MQTT server isn't broken. If the connection is alive, the code calls the `Surfboard.active_instance.build_json_message` method to build the JSON string based on the current values of the `Surfboard` attributes, which are being updated whenever a message with new values arrives from the sensors.

The code saves the JSON string in the `payload` local variable and calls the `pubnub_client.publish` method to publish the `payload` JSON formatted string to the topic name saved in the `pubnub_topic` variable with a QoS level of 0. This way, the message will be published by the thread responsible for processing the MQTT network events for the PubNub MQTT client, and the web-based dashboard that uses the PubNub MQTT server as a data source will be updated. The next line prints a message with the payload that is being published to the PubNub MQTT server.

Running multiple clients

Now, we will run the surfboard sensor emulator and the surfboard monitor we recently coded. Make sure you run these Python programs after you have followed the necessary steps to activate the virtual environment in which we have been working.

Execute the following line to start the surfboard sensor emulator example on any computer or device that you want to use as the MQTT client that works as the surfboard sensor emulator and uses Linux or macOS:

```
python3 surfboard_sensors_emulator.py
```

In Windows, you must execute the following line:

```
python surfboard_sensors_emulator.py
```

After a few seconds, you will see the output shown in the next lines:

```
Result from connect: Connection Accepted.
surfboards/surfboard01/status: 0
surfboards/surfboard01/speedmph: 1.0
surfboards/surfboard01/altitudefeet: 2.0
surfboards/surfboard01/temperaturef: 58.0
surfboards/surfboard01/status: 0
surfboards/surfboard01/speedmph: 1.1
surfboards/surfboard01/altitudefeet: 2.0
surfboards/surfboard01/temperaturef: 58.0
surfboards/surfboard01/status: 1
surfboards/surfboard01/speedmph: 2.0
surfboards/surfboard01/altitudefeet: 3.0
surfboards/surfboard01/temperaturef: 57.0
```

The program will continue publishing messages for the topics to the Mosquitto MQTT server. Keep the code running on your local computer or on the IoT board you have chosen to use as the surfboard sensor emulator for this example.

Then, execute the following line to start the surfboard monitor example on any computer or device that you want to use as the MQTT client that receives messages from the Mosquitto MQTT server and publishes messages to the PubNub MQTT server and uses Linux or macOS:

```
python3 surfboard_monitor.py
```

In Windows, you must execute the following line:

```
python surfboard_monitor.py
```

After a few seconds, you will see an output with messages similar to the next lines. Notice that the values will be different because the time at which you start running the program will make the values vary:

```
Not connected
Result from Mosquitto connect: Connection Accepted.
I've subscribed with QoS: 0
Result from PubNub connect: Connection Accepted.
Message received. Topic: surfboards/surfboard01/status. Payload:
b'3'
Message received. Topic: surfboards/surfboard01/speedmph. Payload:
b'0.0'
Message received. Topic: surfboards/surfboard01/altitudefeet.
Payload: b'3.0'
Message received. Topic: surfboards/surfboard01/temperaturef.
Payload: b'55.0'
Publishing: {"Status": "Ride finished", "Speed MPH": 0.0, "Altitude
Feet": 3.0, "Water Temperature F": 55.0}
Message received. Topic: surfboards/surfboard01/status. Payload:
b'0'
Message received. Topic: surfboards/surfboard01/speedmph. Payload:
b'1.0'
Message received. Topic: surfboards/surfboard01/altitudefeet.
Payload: b'2.0'
Message received. Topic: surfboards/surfboard01/temperaturef.
Payload: b'58.0'
Publishing: {"Status": "Idle", "Speed MPH": 1.0, "Altitude Feet":
2.0, "Water Temperature F": 58.0}
Message received. Topic: surfboards/surfboard01/status. Payload:
b'0'
Message received. Topic: surfboards/surfboard01/speedmph. Payload:
b'1.1'
Message received. Topic: surfboards/surfboard01/altitudefeet.
Payload: b'2.0'
Message received. Topic: surfboards/surfboard01/temperaturef.
Payload: b'58.0'
Publishing: {"Status": "Idle", "Speed MPH": 1.1, "Altitude Feet":
2.0, "Water Temperature F": 58.0}
```

The program will continue receiving messages form the surfboard sensor emulator and publishing messages to the PubNub MQTT server. Keep the code running on your local computer or on the IoT board you have chosen to use as the surfboard monitor for this example.

The following screenshot shows two Terminal windows running on a computer with macOS. The Terminal on the left-hand side is displaying the messages shown by the Python client that works as the surfboard sensor emulator, that is, the surfboard_sensors_emulator.py script. The Terminal on the right-hand side displays the results of running the code for the Python client that works as the surfboard monitor, that is, the surfboard_monitor.py script:

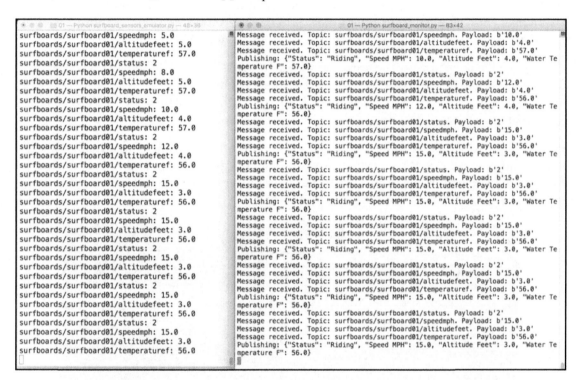

Building a web-based dashboard with freeboard

Now, we are ready to use the PubNub MQTT server as a data source to build a real-time web-based dashboard. As previously explained, we will take advantage of freeboard.io to visualize the surfer and surfboard data in many gauges.

The freeboard.io requires us to sign up and create an account with a valid email and a password before we can build a web-based dashboard. We aren't required to enter any credit card or payment information. If you already have an account at freeboard.io, you can skip the next step.

Go to `http://freeboard.io` in your web browser and click **Start Now**. You can also go straight to `https://freeboard.io/signup`. Enter your desired user name in **Pick a Username**, your email in **Enter Your Email**, and the desired password in **Create a Password**. Once you have filled in all the fields, click **Create My Account**.

Once you have created your account, you can go to `http://freeboard.io` in your web browser and click **Login**. You can achieve the same goal by visiting `https://freeboard.io/login`. Then, enter your user name or email and password, and click **Sign In**. freeboard will display your freeboards, also known as dashboards.

Enter `Surfboard01` in the **enter a name** textbox on the left-hand side of the **Create New** button and then click on this button. freeboard.io will display an empty dashboard with many buttons that allow us to add panes and data sources, among other things. The following screenshot shows the empty dashboard:

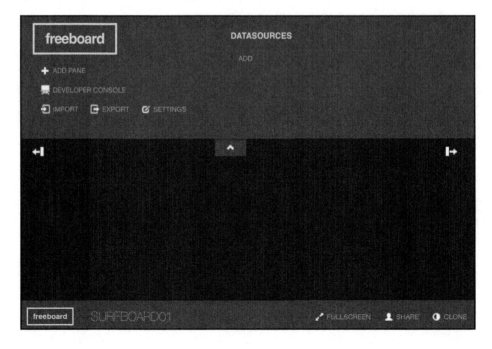

Click on **Add** below **Datasources** and the website will open the **Datasource** dialog box. Select **PubNub** in the **Type** dropdown and the dialog box will display the fields required to define a PubNub datasource.

> Notice that it is also possible to use MQTT as a datasource for freeboard.io. However, this would require us to make our Mosquitto MQTT server publicly available. Instead, we take advantage of the PubNub MQTT interface which allows us to make the messages easily available on the PubNub network. However, you can definitely work with an MQTT server as a datasource in your projects that require a dashboard where freeboard.io provides you the with required features.

Enter surfboard01 in **Name**.

Enter the subscribe key you have copied from the PubNub settings. Remember that the subscribe key is the one that usually starts with the sub-c prefix.

Enter surfboard01 in **Channel**.

If any of the previous value names is wrong, the datasource won't have the appropriate data. The following screenshot shows the configuration for the PubNub datasource with the subscribe displaying only the sub-c prefix:

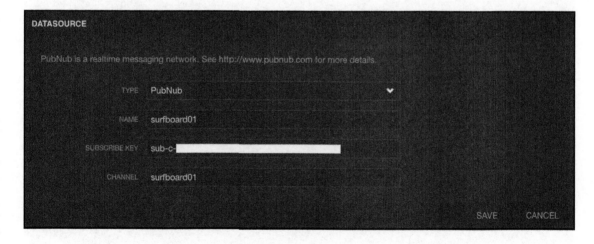

Click **Save** and the datasource will appear listed below **Datasources**. As the surfboard sensor emulator and the surfboard monitor are running, the time shown below **Last Updated** will change every second. If the time doesn't change every second, it means that the datasource has the wrong configuration or that any of the Python programs is not running as expected.

Click on **Add pane** to add a new empty pane to the dashboard. Then, click on the plus sign (+) at the upper right corner of the new empty pane and freeboard will display the **Widget** dialog box.

Select **Text** in the **Type** dropdown and the dialog box will display the fields required to add a text widget to the pane within the dashboard. Enter Status in **Title**.

Click **+ Datasource** on the right-hand side of the **Value** textbox, select **surfboard01**, and then select **Status**. After you make the selections, the following text will appear in the **Value** textbox, datasources ["surfboard01"] ["Status"], as shown in the next screenshot:

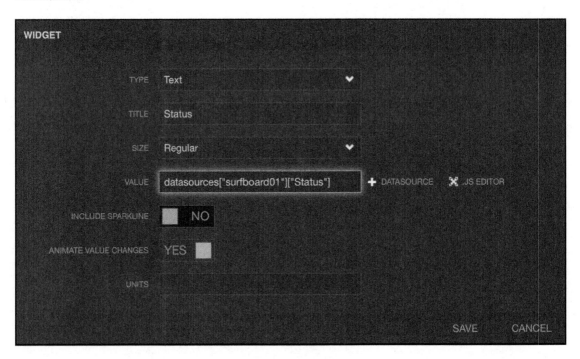

Then, click **Save** and freeboard will close the dialog box and add the new gauge to the previously created pane within the dashboard. The gauge will display the latest value that the surfboard monitor published to the PubNub MQTT interface for the status, that is, the value for the `Status` key in the JSON data that the code has published for the last time. The following screenshot shows the **surfboard01** datasource displaying the last updated time and the gauge showing the latest value for the status:

Click on **Add pane** to add another new empty pane to the dashboard. Then, click on the plus sign (+) at the upper-right corner of the new empty pane and freeboard will display the **Widget** dialog box.

Select **Gauge** in the **Type** dropdown and the dialog box will display the fields required to add a gauge widget to the pane within the dashboard. Enter `Speed` in **Title**.

Click **+ Datasource** at the right-hand side of the **Value** textbox, select **surfboard01**, and then select **Speed MPH**. After you make the selections, the following text will appear in the **Value** textbox: `datasources ["surfboard01"] ["Speed MPH"]`.

Enter `MPH` in **Units**, `0` in **Minimum**, and `40` in **Maximum**. Then, click **Save** and freeboard will close the dialog box and add the new gauge to the previously created pane on the dashboard. The gauge will display the latest value that the surfboard monitor published to the PubNub MQTT interface for the speed, that is, the value for the `Speed MPH` key in the JSON data that the code has published for the last time.

The following screenshot shows the **surfboard01** datasource displaying the last updated time and the added gauge showing the latest value for the speed in mph.

Click on **Add pane** to add another new empty pane to the dashboard. Then, click on the plus sign (+) at the upper-right corner of the new empty pane and freeboard will display the **Widget** dialog box.

Select **Gauge** in the **Type** dropdown and the dialog box will display the fields required to add a gauge widget to the pane on the dashboard. Enter Altitude in **Title**.

Click **+ Datasource** at the right-hand side of the **Value** textbox, select **surfboard01**, and then select **Altitude Feet**. After you make the selections, the following text will appear in the **Value** textbox: datasources ["surfboard01"] ["Altitude Feet"].

Enter Feet in **Units**, 0 in **Minimum**, and 30 in **Maximum**. Then, click **Save** and freeboard will close the dialog box and add the new gauge to the previously created pane on the dashboard. The gauge will display the latest value that the surfboard monitor published to the PubNub MQTT interface for the altitude, that is, the value for the Altitude Feet key in the JSON data that the code has published for the last time.

Now, we will add the last pane. Click on **Add pane** to add another new empty pane to the dashboard. Then, click on the plus sign (**+**) at the upper-right corner of the new empty pane and freeboard will display the **Widget** dialog box.

Select **Gauge** in the **Type** dropdown and the dialog box will display the fields required to add a gauge widget to the pane on the dashboard. Enter Water temperature in **Title**.

Click **+ Datasource** at the right-hand side of the **Value** textbox, select **surfboard01**, and then select **Water Temperature F**. After you make the selections, the following text will appear in the **Value** textbox: datasources ["surfboard01"] ["Water Temperature F"].

Enter ºF in **Units**, 0 in **Minimum**, and 80 in **Maximum**. Then, click **Save** and freeboard will close the dialog box and add the new gauge to the previously created pane on the dashboard. The gauge will display the latest value that the surfboard monitor published to the PubNub MQTT interface for the water temperature, that is, the value for the Water Temperature F key in the JSON data that the code has published for the last time.

Drag and drop the panes to locate the panes with the layout shown in the next screenshot. The screenshot shows the dashboard we built with four panes and three gauges that refresh the data automatically every second when our surfboard monitor publishes data to the PubNub MQTT interface.

We can access the recently built dashboard on any device by entering the URL that our web browser displays at the time we are working with the dashboard. The URL is composed of the `https://freeboard.io/board/` prefix followed by letters and numbers. For example, if the URL is `https://freeboard.io/board/EXAMPLE`, we just need to enter it in any web browser running on any device or computer connected to the internet, and we can watch the gauges and they will be refreshed as new data is being published from our surfboard monitor.

The combination of the PubNub as our datasource and freeboard.io as our web-based dashboard made it easy for us to monitor the data retrieved from the sensors in the surfer's wetsuit and his surfboard. We can monitor the data on any device that provides a web browser. The combination of these two cloud-based services for IoT is just one example of how we can easily combine different services with MQTT in our solutions.

Test your knowledge

Let's see whether you can answer the following questions correctly:

1. The PubNub MQTT interface requires us to use a client ID composed as follows:
    1. `publish_key/subscribe_key/device_id`
    2. `device_id/publish_key/subscribe_key`
    3. `publish_key/device_id`

2. When we publish a message to the PubNub MQTT interface:
    1. It is only available on the PubNub MQTT subnetwork
    2. It becomes available on the PubNub network
    3. It requires a specific payload prefix to become available on the PubNub network

3. Which of the following methods of the `paho.mqtt.client.Client` instance allows us to specify the callback function that the client has to call when it receives a message in a specific topic:
    1. `message_callback_add`
    2. `message_arrived_to_topic_callback`
    3. `message_on_topic`

Summary

In this chapter, we combined everything we learned in the previous chapters to build a web-based dashboard with freeboard that displayed data in gauges every second. We built the solution from scratch. First, we analyzed the requirements and we understood how the IoT board embedded in a surfboard was going to provide us with the necessary data.

We coded a surfboard sensor emulator to work in the same way that the IoT board was working. Then, we configured the PubNub MQTT interface and we coded a surfboard monitor that collected data from the surfboard sensor emulator and published the data to the cloud-based PubNub MQTT interface. We coded a Python program that worked with two MQTT clients with two threaded loop interfaces.

Finally, we could take advantage of the fact that the messages published to the PubNub MQTT interface are also available on the PubNub network to easily build a web-based dashboard with freeboard.

We were able to create code that was capable of running on the most popular and powerful IoT boards. We are ready to use MQTT in all kinds of projects, in one of the most popular and versatile programming languages: Python 3.

Solutions

Chapter 1: Installing an MQTT 3.1.1 Mosquitto server

Questions	Answers
Q1	2
Q2	1
Q3	3
Q4	3
Q5	2

Chapter 2: Using Command-Line and GUI Tools to Learn How MQTT Works

Questions	Answers
Q1	2
Q2	3
Q3	1
Q4	3
Q5	3

Chapter 3: Securing an MQTT 3.1.1 Mosquitto Server

Questions	Answers
Q1	3
Q2	3
Q3	1
Q4	2
Q5	1

Chapter 4: Writing Code to Control a Vehicle with Python and MQTT Messages

Questions	Answers
Q1	1
Q2	2
Q3	2
Q4	2
Q5	3

Chapter 5: Testing and Improving our Vehicle Control Solution in Python

Questions	Answers
Q1	1
Q2	2
Q3	3
Q4	3
Q5	1

Chapter 6: Monitoring a Surfing Competition with Cloud-Based Real-Time MQTT Providers and Python

Questions	Answers
Q1	1
Q2	2
Q3	1

Other Books You May Enjoy

If you enjoyed this book, you may be interested in these other books by Packt:

Mastering Python Networking
Eric Chou

ISBN: 978-1-78439-700-5

- Review all the fundamentals of Python and the TCP/IP suite
- Use Python to execute commands when the device does not support the API or programmatic interaction with the device
- Implement automation techniques by integrating Python with Cisco, Juniper, and Arista eAPI
- Integrate Ansible using Python to control Cisco, Juniper, and Arista networks
- Achieve network security with Python
- Build Flask-based web-service APIs with Python
- Construct a Python-based migration plan from a legacy to scalable SDN-based network.

Python Network Programming Cookbook - Second Edition
Pradeeban Kathiravelu, Dr. M. O. Faruque Sarker

ISBN: 978-1-78646-399-9

- Develop TCP/IP networking client/server applications
- Administer local machines' IPv4/IPv6 network interfaces
- Write multi-purpose efficient web clients for HTTP and HTTPS protocols
- Perform remote system administration tasks over Telnet and SSH connections
- Interact with popular websites via web services such as XML-RPC, SOAP, and REST APIs
- Monitor and analyze major common network security vulnerabilities
- Develop Software-Defined Networks with Ryu, OpenDaylight, Floodlight, ONOS, and POX Controllers
- Emulate simple and complex networks with Mininet and its extensions for network and systems emulations
- Learn to configure and build network systems and Virtual Network Functions (VNF) in heterogeneous deployment environments
- Explore various Python modules to program the Internet

Leave a review - let other readers know what you think

Please share your thoughts on this book with others by leaving a review on the site that you bought it from. If you purchased the book from Amazon, please leave us an honest review on this book's Amazon page. This is vital so that other potential readers can see and use your unbiased opinion to make purchasing decisions, we can understand what our customers think about our products, and our authors can see your feedback on the title that they have worked with Packt to create. It will only take a few minutes of your time, but is valuable to other potential customers, our authors, and Packt. Thank you!

Index

public key infrastructure (PKI) 71
publish-subscribe pattern
    working with 10, 12, 13
publisher 11
PubNub MQTT bridge
    reference 18
PubNub MQTT interface
    configuring 182, 183
PubNub
    reference 176
Python 3.6x
    virtual environment, creating with 107
Python
    commands, processing 141, 142, 144, 146, 148
    messages, receiving in 130, 132, 135
    messages, sending with 148, 151
    paho-mqtt, installing for 115, 116
    used, for subscribing topics 122, 123

Q

QoS levels
    about 54
    at least once delivery 55
    at most once delivery 55
    exactly once delivery 55
    overhead 64

R

retained last will messages
    working with 161, 163, 164

S

Secure Socket Layers (SSL) 69
subscribers 11
Surfboard monitor 177
surfboard sensor emulator
    about 177
    coding 177, 178, 179, 182

T

testament feature
    working with 155, 158, 159, 161
threadedclient interface
    using 168, 169
TLS client certificate authentication
    configuring, in Mosquitto 93
TLS protocol version
    forcing, to specific number 100
TLS transport security
    configuring, in Mosquitto 79, 80
topic subscription
    with command-line tool 36, 37
    with GUI tool 38, 40, 41
    with Python 122, 123
topics
    best practices 51, 52
    defining 105, 174
    unsubscribing, with GUI tool 47, 48, 49, 50
Transport Layer Security (TLS) 69

U

unmanned aerial vehicle (UAV) 36

V

virtual environment
    activating 111, 112, 113
    creating, with PEP 405 107
    creating, with Python 3.6.x 107
    deactivating 114
    directory structure 109, 110
virtual private network (VPN) 69
virtualenv
    reference 107

W

web-based dashboard
    building, with freeboard 197, 199, 200, 202
Windows
    Mosquitto server, installing on 28, 30

Printed in Great Britain
by Amazon

84615095R00133